Moving for Injunctive Relief

4TH EDITION 2021

Brandon F. White, Esq.

2220190B04

Printed in the United States of America

This publication should be cited: *Moving for Injunctive Relief* (MCLE, Inc. 2021)

Library of Congress Control Number: 2021949341
ISBN: 9781683453093

Massachusetts Continuing Legal Education, Inc.
Ten Winter Place, Boston, MA 02108-4751
800-966-6253 | Fax 617-482-9498 | www.mcle.org

ACKNOWLEDGMENTS

The content of this book was first published as Chapter 5 in the *Massachusetts Superior Court Civil Practice Manual,* now in its 5th Edition 2021. With the intention to develop a monograph for practitioners whose Superior Court practice includes moving for injunctive relief, MCLE has issued this fourth edition book. MCLE is grateful to its author, Brandon F. White, for his original work on the manual. The judicial commentary that appears in this book was provided by the Hon. Paul A. Chernoff and the Hon. Stephen E. Neel for the 2002 Supplement to the manual, and Bruce T. Eisenhut, Esq. kindly provided the book's ethics commentary..

Maryanne G. Jensen, Esq.
Director of Publications
October 2021

INTRODUCTION

This MCLE publication presents the strategies, steps, and practice tips crucial to obtaining injunctive relief for your client. Covering the sequence of events from the initial client interview to the hearing, *Moving for Injunctive Relief* contains practical advice on ex parte temporary restraining orders, temporary restraining orders, and preliminary injunctions. It provides particularly helpful guidance on such issues as determining whether to seek injunctive relief, drafting injunction pleadings, courtroom procedures, service of process, interlocutory appeal, and enforcement of the injunction. The exhibits, which were selected to illustrate all phases of injunctive relief, provide samples of the type of precise language necessary for success in this area of practice. Written by an experienced litigator, this publication offers valuable information on injunctive relief in Massachusetts for both beginning and seasoned civil litigators.

ABOUT THE AUTHOR

BRANDON F. WHITE is a partner of Foley Hoag LLP in Boston. He concentrates on securities fraud, fiduciary duty, and corporate governance issues. Previously, he clerked for the chief justice of the Massachusetts Supreme Judicial Court. He is a graduate of Boston College Law School and Boston College.

TABLE OF CONTENTS

Chapter 1   When to Seek Immediate Injunctive Relief

§ 1.1   Introduction 1–1
§ 1.2   Initial Investigation 1–1
§ 1.3   Standard for Preliminary Injunctive Relief 1–2
§ 1.4   Determining Whether to Seek a Preliminary Injunction 1–3
§ 1.5   Temporary Restraining Order Versus Preliminary Injunction 1–5
EXHIBIT 1A—Motion for a Temporary Restraining Order 1–8
EXHIBIT 1B—Motion for Preliminary Injunction 1–12

Chapter 2   Preparing the Injunction Papers

§ 2.1   Introduction 2–1
§ 2.2   Verified Complaint.. 2–2
§ 2.3   Supporting Affidavits.. 2–3
§ 2.4   Motion for a Preliminary Injunction and Proposed Order 2–4
§ 2.5   Memorandum in Support of Motion for Preliminary Injunction 2–5
§ 2.6   Motion for Short Order of Notice.............................. 2–7
§ 2.7   Motion for Special Process Server 2–7
EXHIBIT 2A—Verified Complaint 2–8
EXHIBIT 2B—Motion for a Short Order of Notice................. 2–15
EXHIBIT 2C—Motion for Appointment of a Special Process Server 2–17

Chapter 3   Filing the Injunction Papers

§ 3.1   The Filing Procedure... 3–1

Chapter 4   Opposing a Motion for a Preliminary Injunction

§ 4.1   Initial Considerations 4–1
§ 4.2   Standstill Agreement.. 4–3
§ 4.3   Opposition Affidavits... 4–3
§ 4.4   Opposition Memorandum.. 4–4
EXHIBIT 4A—Standstill Agreement...................................... 4–6

Chapter 5   Preliminary Injunction Hearing

§ 5.1   Preparing for the Hearing.. 5–1
§ 5.1.1   Arrange to Have Your Client Present 5–1
§ 5.1.2   Arrive Early at the Court............................. 5–2
§ 5.1.3   Consider the Need to File Rebuttal Affidavits or a Supplemental Memorandum 5–2

§ 5.1.4   Consider How You Are Going to Handle
           the Security Issue 5–2
§ 5.1.5   Bring to Court Extra Copies of All of
           the Filed Papers 5–3
§ 5.1.6   Prepare Your Oral Argument 5–3

Chapter 6   After the Hearing
§ 6.1   What to Do Prior to the Court's Decision 6–1
§ 6.2   What to Do if the Preliminary Injunction Is Allowed .. 6–1
§ 6.3   Appealing the Grant or Denial of a Preliminary
         Injunction 6–2
§ 6.4   Enforcement of a Preliminary Injunction 6–3

Chapter 7   Seeking Injunctive Relief in Particular Situations
§ 7.1   Enforcement of Employee Noncompetition
         Agreements 7–1
         § 7.1.1   Enforceability of the Noncompetition
                    Agreement 7–2
         § 7.1.2   Costs and Benefits of Litigation 7–3
         § 7.1.3   Settlement 7–4
         § 7.1.4   Protective Order 7–4
         § 7.1.5   Determining Who the Defendants
                    Should Be 7–5
         § 7.1.6   Injunction Bonds 7–5
         § 7.1.7   Documents in the Possession
                    of the Former Employee 7–5
§ 7.2   Enforcement of Statutes by the Attorney General 7–5
EXHIBIT 7A—Confidentiality Stipulation 7–7

Table of Cases

Table of Statutes, Rules, and References

Index

ELECTRONIC FORMS DOWNLOAD

All of the exhibits from this book are available for download from the MCLE website. **You must be signed into the account used to purchase this book to access the downloadable forms.**

To download the forms, go to

www.mcle.org/forms

and enter Forms Download Code (case sensitive):

43M5UFm3

This code applies only to the 4th Edition of *Moving for Injunctive Relief.* You may select all forms to download or only those you need, and may return to the download page anytime while this edition remains in print.

Use Note:

These forms are electronic versions of the exhibits as they appear in the book—there is no interactive software that deletes information or fills in blank lines. After downloading, you can modify text-based exhibits with your word processing software, manipulating the text, spacing (e.g., tab settings, margins), and typographical format (e.g., underlining, italicizing) as needed. **Some files (e.g., official court forms) are embedded as images in Word files. These files cannot be edited with Word.** Please bear in mind that forms in MCLE publications are examples only. Practitioners must check original sources of authority for current law and adapt forms to fit specific case facts and individual needs. For court forms and other standardized forms, be sure to check with the original source to obtain the most recent version and any special instructions.

If you have any questions or problems accessing your forms download, please contact MCLE's Customer Service at **customerservice@mcle.org** or by phone at 1-800-966-6253.

CHAPTER 1

When to Seek Immediate Injunctive Relief

Brandon F. White, Esq.
Foley Hoag LLP, Boston

§ 1.1   Introduction 1–1
§ 1.2   Initial Investigation.. 1–1
§ 1.3   Standard for Preliminary Injunctive Relief 1–2
§ 1.4   Determining Whether to Seek a Preliminary Injunction 1–3
§ 1.5   Temporary Restraining Order Versus Preliminary Injunction 1–5
EXHIBIT 1A—Motion for a Temporary Restraining Order 1–8
EXHIBIT 1B—Motion for Preliminary Injunction 1–12

§ 1.1   INTRODUCTION

A key employee leaves a company and starts a competitive business in violation of a noncompetition agreement. A business partner threatens to deplete the partnership's bank account and leave the state. A municipality informs a residential property owner that it is about to demolish her home.

In these and other situations, your client will demand immediate injunctive relief. Your client will want you to respond quickly and effectively to the legal emergency. If immediate injunctive relief is not obtained, your client may suffer irreparable harm that a later award of money damages will not remedy.

What do you do when confronted with these situations? This chapter discusses temporary restraining orders and preliminary injunctions and how you can obtain them and oppose them in the Superior Court. The chapter also addresses enforcement of employee noncompetition agreements and injunctions obtained by the Massachusetts Office of the Attorney General.

§ 1.2   INITIAL INVESTIGATION

Because of the emergency nature of these cases, it is easy to forego the careful factual and legal investigation of a claim that should always precede filing a lawsuit. You should resist the impulse to conduct a cursory and incomplete investigation.

Judicial Commentary
It is worth the preparation time because, realistically, you usually have only one shot at equitable relief. Few injunction cases ever go to an evidentiary hearing or trial. The resolution of the preliminary relief issue, one way or the other, normally disposes of the case.

Interview the client thoroughly about the facts of the case. Speak with other witnesses if they are available. Review all relevant documents. Consider the applicable law and legal theories. The purpose of this initial investigation is to ensure that you have a meritorious case, that you have good grounds to seek preliminary injunctive relief, and that you do not make any significant mistakes that will haunt you later during the litigation.

Ethics Commentary
For an excellent discussion of the safeguards that an attorney should take to avoid unjustifiable reliance on the client's version of the facts, see Margaret D. Xifaras, "The Attorney-Client Relationship," *Ethical Lawyering in Massachusetts* ch. 4 (MCLE, Inc. 5th ed. 2021).

§ 1.3   STANDARD FOR PRELIMINARY INJUNCTIVE RELIEF

The requirements for preliminary injunctive relief in Massachusetts are well established. The court must consider the following three factors:

- the plaintiff's likelihood of success on the merits,

- the risk of irreparable harm to the plaintiff if the injunction is not issued, and

- the irreparable harm to be suffered by the moving party compared to the harm to the defendant if the injunction is issued.

Packaging Indus. Grp., Inc. v. Cheney, 380 Mass. 609, 617 (1980).

Under Massachusetts law, the public interest ordinarily is not considered in determining whether to grant a preliminary injunction. *Bank of New Eng. v. Mortg. Corp. of New Eng.*, 30 Mass. App. Ct. 238, 245 (1991). In certain cases, however, the public interest will be a fourth factor weighed by the court. *Planned Parenthood League of Mass., Inc. v. Operation Rescue*, 406 Mass. 701, 716 (1990). In cases where a party seeks to enjoin governmental action, the judge must also determine if the relief sought promotes the public interest or at least will not adversely affect the public. *Bos. Police Patrolmen's Ass'n, Inc. v. Police Dep't of Bos.*, 446 Mass. 46, 50–51 (2006); *Tri-Nel Mgmt., Inc. v. Bd. of Health*, 433 Mass. 217 (2001). Courts may also consider the public interest when a public entity is involved or when the substantive law concerns the public interest. *Hull Mun. Lighting Plant v. Mass. Mun. Wholesale Elec. Co.*, 399 Mass. 640, 648 (1987); *Bank of New Eng. v. Mortg. Corp. of New Eng.*, 30 Mass. App. Ct. at 246.

Massachusetts courts employ a "balancing" test in evaluating these factors. If failure to issue the injunction would subject the plaintiff to substantial risk of irreparable harm, the court must then balance this risk against any similar risk of harm that granting the injunction would create for the defendant. *Packaging Indus. Grp. v. Cheney*, 380 Mass. at 617. As the Supreme Judicial Court has explained: "What matters as to each party is not the raw amount of irreparable harm the party might conceivably suffer, but rather the risk of such harm in light of the party's success on the merits." *Packaging Indus. Grp. v. Cheney*, 380 Mass. at 617. Only where the balance between these risks cuts in favor of the moving party may a preliminary injunction properly issue. *Packaging Indus. Grp. v. Cheney*, 380 Mass. at 617. Courts will not reach this balancing test, however, if plaintiffs cannot first show a likelihood of succeeding on their claims. *Garcia v. Dep't of Hous. & Cmty. Dev.*, 480 Mass. 736, 761 (2018).

Judicial Commentary

The plaintiff's pleadings will be read first, and the plaintiff will argue first. Acknowledge competing risks up front and suggest ways in which the opposition's risks can be minimized.

"Irreparable harm" in the context of a preliminary injunction is harm that cannot be vindicated by a final judgment. *Packaging Indus. Grp. v. Cheney*, 380 Mass. at 617 n.11. Usually, monetary losses are not considered irreparable harm. *Norfolk Cty. Hosp. v. Commonwealth*, 25 Mass. App. Ct. 586, 593 (1988). Examples of irreparable harm include loss of trade secrets or loss of goodwill. Although economic loss alone does not ordinarily rise to the level of irreparable harm, in some circumstances courts will find irreparable harm even if monetary damages are involved. *Hull Mun. Lighting Plant v. Mass. Mun. Wholesale Elec. Co.*, 399 Mass. 640, 643 (1987). Specifically, courts have recognized two exceptions: (1) "where the moving party has shown that the risk of loss of monetary damages 'threatens the very existence of the movant's business,' and (2) where 'the defendant is insolvent or its assets are in danger of depletion and dissipation.'" *Paypal, Inc. v. NantHealth, Inc.*, 2020 Mass. Super. LEXIS 38, Op. No. 144450, at *2–3 (Mass. Super. Ct. Feb. 7, 2020) (quoting *Hull Mun. Lighting Plant v. Mass. Mun. Wholesale Elec. Co.*, 399 Mass. at 643); *Fleet Nat'l Bank v. Rapid Reprocessing Co., Inc.*, 643 F. Supp. 1065, 1066 (D. Mass. 1986).

§ 1.4   DETERMINING WHETHER TO SEEK A PRELIMINARY INJUNCTION

The decision to seek a preliminary injunction can be one of the most significant strategic decisions in a case. Success or failure at this stage of the proceedings can control the ultimate outcome of the litigation. As a result, you should consider the following factors carefully.

First, do the facts of your case satisfy the standard for entry of a preliminary injunction? Are you able to demonstrate a strong likelihood of success on the merits, irreparable harm if the injunction is not issued, and little or no harm to the defendant if the injunction is issued? If your case for a preliminary injunction is weak, you should consider whether it makes sense to risk the loss of an important motion early in your case. In cases where an immediate preliminary injunction might not be appropriate, you may consider moving for expedited discovery and seeking a preliminary injunction *after* you have had the opportunity to discover additional facts—through depositions or documents—that bolster your case.

Alternatively, you might consider consolidating the preliminary injunction hearing with the trial on the merits after conducting some limited discovery. Mass. R. Civ. P. 65(b)(2); *see PC-Plus Techs., Inc. v. Gokani*, 10 Mass. L. Rptr. 175 (Mass. Super. Ct. Apr. 14, 1999) (Fecteau, J.) (ordered consolidation of motion for preliminary injunction with trial on merits in action to enforce employee noncompetition agreement). Your client has the right to waive a jury, but if your opponent has requested a jury trial you may not be able to achieve consolidation. Mass. R. Civ. P. 65(b)(2).

Judicial Commentary

The passage of time invariably weakens your prayer for injunctive relief. Be prepared to explain to the judge any delay in seeking relief. It is unusual for a judge to allow a motion to consolidate the preliminary injunction hearing with the trial on the merits (because that would involve jumping ahead of hundreds of older cases in the session) unless your reasons are compelling. Be aware, however, that it is not unheard of for a judge to announce sua sponte such a consolidation.

Practice Note

A plaintiff who can afford to wait long enough to take some discovery, and who needs information from other sources to support the motion, may apply for targeted expedited discovery preceding the preliminary injunction hearing. A defendant may seek discovery to obtain evidence for use in opposing the motion. Be careful about agreeing to expedited discovery and a delayed preliminary injunction hearing or trial. Discovery delays or the court's own schedule may make it necessary to reschedule the hearing or trial. As a result, the hearing or trial may occur several weeks or months after the date originally agreed to by the parties.

Second, can your client afford the substantial investment of time and money that a preliminary injunction motion may require, and the risk that a preliminary injunction may not issue? In some cases, it is more cost-effective to forego the preliminary injunction hearing and either consolidate the preliminary hearing with the trial or move for a speedy trial.

Third, can your client afford an injunction bond if the preliminary injunction is entered? Rule 65(c) of the Massachusetts Rules of Civil Procedure provides that the court should require security if a preliminary injunction issues unless "good cause" is shown for waiving it. The purpose of security is to provide the defendant a remedy if it subsequently should be determined that the court improperly issued the preliminary injunction. In the absence of such security, a defendant who is wrongfully enjoined is not entitled to recover for losses resulting from the injunction. *All Stainless, Inc. v. Colby*, 364 Mass. 773, 782 (1974). The amount of the security should cover the costs (usually not attorney fees) and pecuniary injury that may accrue during the period of the injunction. *O'Day v. Theran*, 7 Mass. App. Ct. 622, 625 (1979). Although the court need not require a bond, and the amount lies within the judge's discretion, you should discuss this bond provision with your client *before* seeking a preliminary injunction.

Judicial Commentary

Use your imagination to suggest innovative and meaningful substitutes for traditional security, such as installment payments into an escrow account, agreements not to encumber or transfer certain property, or expedited discovery and other concessions. Remember—this is equity.

Ethics Commentary

Counsel should be careful that innovative substitutes are realistic and the client will comply. For a case where the client did not comply with a substitute arrangement for security and the lawyer, perhaps out of embarrassment, lied to opposing counsel and a court-appointed master as to his client's noncompliance, see *In re Joyce*, 13 Mass. Att'y Disc. R. 302 (1997) (one-year suspension).

Your client can seek a preliminary injunction even if subject to an agreement to resolve the merits of any dispute by arbitration. Arbitration agreements are favored and are commonly enforced by Massachusetts courts, but arbitration panels have traditionally not been equipped to handle preliminary injunction or temporary restraining order motions, so Massachusetts courts have heard them in aid of arbitration. The court's evaluation of the likelihood of success on the merits is compatible with arbitration because the court's evaluation is not based on a full presentation of the facts and leaves final resolution of the merits to the arbitration. *Hull Mun. Lighting Plant v. Mass. Mun. Wholesale Elec. Co.*, 399 Mass. 640, 648–49 (1987).

§ 1.5 TEMPORARY RESTRAINING ORDER VERSUS PRELIMINARY INJUNCTION

Because of the relative ease with which one can obtain a prompt hearing on a preliminary injunction motion, the plaintiff will often bypass seeking a temporary restraining order (TRO) and proceed directly to seeking a short order of notice for hearing on a preliminary injunction. There are, however, certain circumstances where you should consider seeking a TRO, such as the following:

- where immediate relief is essential and you cannot wait four to seven days for the preliminary injunction hearing (e.g., the ball and crane are about to destroy your client's building); and

- where ex parte relief is essential and you need to obtain an injunction without first providing notice to the defendant (e.g., you are seeking to freeze the defendant's assets and there is a risk that the defendant will conceal or transfer assets if provided with prior notice).

The standard of proof for an ex parte TRO is different from that required for a preliminary injunction or a TRO sought with notice. See **Exhibits 1A** and **1B**.

> A temporary restraining order may be granted without written or oral notice to the adverse party or his attorney only if it clearly appears from specific facts shown by affidavit or by the verified complaint that immediate and irreparable injury, loss or damage will result to the applicant before the adverse party or his attorney can be heard in opposition.

Mass. R. Civ. P. 65(a). A preliminary injunction will not be issued without notice to the adverse party. Mass. R. Civ. P. 65(b)(1). See **Exhibit 5B**.

Judicial Commentary

Ex parte equitable relief is viewed with some suspicion by judges—especially requests made on the Friday afternoon of a holiday weekend. It will bolster your credibility if you can represent to the judge that you tried to contact opposing counsel or that you asked the other side to maintain the status quo for a few days. It is possible that you will not receive a hearing on an application for an ex parte TRO. Instead, the judge may rule on the papers.

Note the difference between a TRO with notice and an ex parte TRO. Whenever possible, notify the other side that you are going to court.

Think about alternative relief as a fallback position if you think the court may be reluctant to give the relief requested. The court may be willing to grant your client something less than the initial relief requested. Often, it is better to get something less rather than nothing at all.

Practice Note

Superior Court judges will rarely grant a TRO in the absence of notice to the defendant. Accordingly, you should seek an ex parte TRO only in the rare circumstance where such extraordinary relief is essential. Otherwise, your client will risk an early litigation defeat—with all of the negative baggage that goes along with it.

While a preliminary injunction ordinarily remains in place until final judgment (or settlement), a TRO initially cannot exceed ten days in duration. A court may, however, extend a TRO by an additional ten-day period "for good cause shown." Mass. R. Civ. P. 65(a). If a TRO is granted without notice, the application for a preliminary injunction shall be set down for hearing at the earliest possible time, and in any event within ten days. Mass. R. Civ. P. 65(a).

If a TRO is entered against your client, you may move to dissolve or modify the TRO with two days' notice, unless a shorter notice period is prescribed by the court. Mass. R. Civ. P. 65(a). You should, however, carefully consider whether you want to exercise your right to such prompt reconsideration of the TRO. In many instances, the preliminary injunction hearing will be scheduled within days, and your time could be served more profitably by preparing a compelling presentation to defeat the preliminary injunction motion.

Judicial Commentary

If you desire an evidentiary hearing, you may want to forego a TRO request. You stand a better chance for an evidentiary hearing at the preliminary injunction stage than at the time of a TRO request.

EXHIBIT 1A—Motion for a Temporary Restraining Order

COMMONWEALTH OF MASSACHUSETTS

MIDDLESEX, ss.   SUPERIOR COURT
                                                      CIVIL ACTION NO.

COMPUTER SOFTWARE, INC.,	)
Plaintiff	)
	)
v.	)
	)
HARRY ADAMS and KOPY SOFTWARE, INC.,	)
	)
Defendants	)

PLAINTIFF'S EMERGENCY MOTION
FOR A TEMPORARY RESTRAINING ORDER

Pursuant to Mass. R. Civ. P. 65(a), Plaintiff Computer Software, Inc. ("CSI") moves for a temporary restraining order against Defendants Harry Adams ("Adams") and Kopy Software, Inc. ("KSI") that will enjoin and restrain Defendants and their agents, servants, employees and attorneys from (a) causing or allowing Adams to work for or on behalf of KSI prior to October 28, 2014 and (b) disclosing or using any of CSI's trade secrets or confidential business information. A temporary restraining order is required because CSI learned yesterday that Adams has commenced employment with KSI, one of CSI's direct competitors, in violation of his one-year noncompete agreement. If a temporary restraining order is not entered, CSI will suffer irreparable injury because its trade secrets, confidential business information and customer goodwill will be jeopardized.

In further support thereof, CSI states as follows:

1. CSI designs, programs, markets and installs computer software for use by businesses engaged in the distribution of products. CSI's proprietary and confidential software includes computer programs for inventory management, sales order management, financial management, and other business functions.

2. CSI and KSI are direct competitors. Like CSI, KSI designs, programs, markets and installs computer software for use by businesses engaged in the distribution of products. Like CSI, KSI markets computer programs for inventory management, sales order management, financial management, and

other business functions. Like CSI, KSI operates on Digital Equipment Corporation's VAX hardware and utilizes Digital's VMS operating system. Like CSI, KSI has offices in the Boston area and in Palo Alto, and markets its software throughout the United States. Like CSI, KSI markets its software to large companies with annual revenues exceeding $500 million. As a result, KSI and CSI frequently compete for the same customers.

3.   Adams was employed as a software programmer by CSI for almost nine years. During his employment, he spent literally hundreds of hours mastering the operational and functional features and limitations of CSI's proprietary and confidential software. In addition, he used and became familiar with other CSI confidential information, including: the manner in which the computer software is installed at a customer's site; the prices, terms and conditions of CSI's contracts with customers; its pricing and price lists; and its financial information. He also had contacts with and became familiar with certain of CSI's customers.

4.   Adams signed an Employment Agreement with CSI that included a one-year noncompetition provision and a nondisclosure provision. The Agreement provided that "the Employee understands and agrees that the Company will suffer irreparable harm in the event that the Employee fails to comply with the obligations of this Agreement, and that monetary damages will be inadequate to compensate the Company for such breach. Accordingly, the Employee agrees that the Company will, in addition to any other remedies available to it at law or in equity, be entitled to injunctive relief to enforce the terms of this Agreement."

5.   Adams voluntarily resigned from CSI on October 4, 2014 and, in violation of his contractual obligations to CSI, assumed a new position as a Software Programmer for KSI.

6.   CSI has demonstrated both a probability of success on the merits and irreparable harm if the restraining order is not granted. The noncompetition and nondisclosure provisions are enforceable to protect CSI's trade secrets, confidential business information and goodwill. In the absence of injunctive relief, CSI will suffer irreparable harm because it will lose its confidential information, and its customer relationships will be irreparably harmed.

7.   Defendants will not suffer any irreparable harm if the restraining order is allowed. Adams voluntarily signed the Employment Agreement, he voluntarily resigned from CSI, and he knowingly joined a competitor. He knew, or should have known, that CSI would seek enforcement of its Agreement to protect its confidential information and goodwill. KSI knew, or should have known, of the Employment Agreement because, among other things, CSI sent a copy of it to KSI.

8.   The public interest will be served by enforcement of the Agreement's noncompetition and nondisclosure provisions. High technology companies such

as CSI must protect their confidential information and customer goodwill in order to remain competitive. If provisions such as those involved here are not enforced by the courts, the public interest will be thwarted.

9. Accordingly, based on the Verified Complaint, Affidavit of Samuel Goodright, and Memorandum of Law, Plaintiff CSI respectfully moves that the Court enter the requested temporary restraining order, attached hereto as Exhibit A.

COMPUTER SOFTWARE, INC.
By its Attorneys,

_____
Attorney(s) (BBO No. XXXXXX)
Firm Name
Address
Phone

Dated:

CERTIFICATE OF SERVICE

I hereby certify that the above document is being served within the time required by Superior Court Standing Order No. 1-88 except as modified by the Session Judge or by the Regional Administrative Justice. I further certify that I served a true copy of this document upon the attorney of record for each party by hand/mail on [date].

_____

EXHIBIT A

COMMONWEALTH OF MASSACHUSETTS

MIDDLESEX, ss.   SUPERIOR COURT
                                                        CIVIL ACTION NO.

COMPUTER SOFTWARE, INC., Plaintiff	))))
v.	))
HARRY ADAMS and KOPY SOFTWARE, INC.,	))
Defendants	))

TEMPORARY RESTRAINING ORDER

After hearing, the Court hereby ENJOINS and RESTRAINS Defendants Harry Adams ("Adams") and Kopy Software, Inc. ("KSI") and their agents, servants, employees and attorneys, until 5:00 p.m. on October 28, 2014, from (a) causing or allowing Adams to work for or on behalf of KSI; and (b) disclosing or using any of the trade secrets or confidential business information of Computer Software, Inc. ("CSI"), including, without limitation: CSI's source and object code for its computer software; information regarding the operational and functional features and limitations of CSI's computer software; the manner in which CSI's computer software is installed at a customer's site; the prices, terms and conditions of CSI's contracts with its customers; CSI's pricing and price lists; and CSI's financial information.

The Court further orders that a preliminary injunction hearing in this matter be scheduled for October 28, 2014 at 2:00 p.m.

Dated: _____   _____
                                      (_____, J.)

EXHIBIT 1B—Motion for Preliminary Injunction

COMMONWEALTH OF MASSACHUSETTS

MIDDLESEX, ss.   SUPERIOR COURT
                                                        CIVIL ACTION NO.

COMPUTER SOFTWARE, INC., Plaintiff v. HARRY ADAMS and KOPY SOFTWARE, INC., Defendants	)))))))))))

PLAINTIFF'S EMERGENCY MOTION
FOR A PRELIMINARY INJUNCTION

Pursuant to Mass. R. Civ. P. 65(b), Plaintiff Computer Software, Inc. ("CSI") moves for a preliminary injunction against Defendants Harry Adams ("Adams") and Kopy Software, Inc. ("KSI") that will enjoin and restrain Defendants and their agents, servants, employees and attorneys from (a) causing or allowing Adams to work for or on behalf of KSI prior to October 4, 2015 and (b) disclosing or using any of CSI's trade secrets or confidential business information.

In support thereof, CSI states as follows:

1. CSI designs, programs, markets and installs computer software for use by businesses engaged in the distribution of products. CSI's proprietary and confidential software includes computer programs for inventory management, sales order management, financial management, and other business functions.

2. CSI and KSI are direct competitors. Like CSI, KSI designs, programs, markets and installs computer software for use by businesses engaged in the distribution of products. Like CSI, KSI markets computer programs for inventory management, sales order management, financial management, and other business functions. Like CSI, KSI operates on Digital Equipment Corporation's VAX hardware and utilizes Digital's VMS operating system. Like CSI, KSI has offices in the Boston area and in Palo Alto, and markets its software throughout the United States. Like CSI, KSI markets its software to large companies with annual revenues exceeding $500 million. As a result, KSI and CSI frequently compete for the same customers.

3. Adams was employed as a software programmer by CSI for almost nine years. During his employment he spent literally hundreds of hours mastering the operational and functional features and limitations of CSI's proprietary and confidential software. In addition, he used and became familiar with other CSI confidential information, including the manner in which the computer software is installed at a customer's site; the prices, terms and conditions of CSI's contracts with customers; its pricing and price lists; and its financial information. He also had contacts with and became familiar with certain of CSI's customers.

4. Adams signed an Employment Agreement with CSI that included a one-year noncompetition provision and a nondisclosure provision. The Agreement provided that "the Employee understands and agrees that the Company will suffer irreparable harm in the event that the Employee fails to comply with the obligations of this Agreement, and that monetary damages will be inadequate to compensate the Company for such breach. Accordingly, the Employee agrees that the Company will, in addition to any other remedies available to it at law or in equity, be entitled to injunctive relief to enforce the terms of this Agreement."

5. Adams voluntarily resigned from CSI on October 4, 2014 and, in violation of his contractual obligations to CSI, assumed a new position as a Software Programmer for KSI.

6. CSI has demonstrated both a probability of success on the merits and irreparable harm if the injunction is not granted. The noncompetition and nondisclosure provisions are enforceable to protect CSI's trade secrets, confidential business information and goodwill. In the absence of injunctive relief, CSI will suffer irreparable harm because it will lose its confidential information, and its customer relationships will be irreparably harmed.

7. Defendants will not suffer any irreparable harm if the injunction is allowed. Adams voluntarily signed the Employment Agreement, he voluntarily resigned from CSI, and he knowingly joined a competitor. He knew, or should have known, that CSI would seek enforcement of its Agreement in order to protect its confidential information and goodwill. KSI knew, or should have known, of the Employment Agreement because, among other things, CSI sent a copy of it to KSI.

8. The public interest will be served by enforcement of the Agreement's noncompetition and nondisclosure provisions. High technology companies such as CSI must protect their confidential information and customer goodwill in order to remain competitive. If provisions such as those involved here are not enforced by the courts, the public interest will be thwarted.

9. Accordingly, based on the Verified Complaint, Affidavit of Samuel Goodright, and Memorandum of Law to be submitted at the hearing, Plaintiff CSI

respectfully moves that the Court enter the requested preliminary injunction, attached hereto as Exhibit A.

COMPUTER SOFTWARE, INC.
By its Attorneys,

_____
Attorney(s) (BBO No. XXXXXX)
Firm Name
Address
Phone

Dated:

CERTIFICATE OF SERVICE

I hereby certify that the above document is being served within the time required by Superior Court Standing Order No. No. 1-88 except as modified by the Session Judge or by the Regional Administrative Justice. I further certify that I served a true copy of this document upon the attorney of record for each party by hand/mail on [date].

_____

EXHIBIT A

COMMONWEALTH OF MASSACHUSETTS

MIDDLESEX, ss.   SUPERIOR COURT
                                                  CIVIL ACTION NO.

COMPUTER SOFTWARE, INC., Plaintiff	)
	)
	)
	)
v.	)
	)
HARRY ADAMS and KOPY SOFTWARE, INC.,	)
	)
Defendants	)
	)

PRELIMINARY INJUNCTION

After hearing, the Court hereby ENJOINS and RESTRAINS Defendants Harry Adams ("Adams") and Kopy Software, Inc. ("KSI") and their agents, servants, employees and attorneys from (a) causing or allowing Adams to work for or on behalf of KSI prior to October 4, 2015; and (b) disclosing or using any of the trade secrets or confidential business information of Computer Software, Inc. ("CSI"), including, without limitation: CSI's source and object code for its computer software; information regarding the operational and functional features and limitations of CSI's computer software; the manner in which CSI's computer software is installed at a customer's site; the prices, terms and conditions of CSI's contracts with its customers; CSI's pricing and price lists; and CSI's financial information.

Dated: _____   _____
                                   (_____, J.)

CHAPTER 2

Preparing the Injunction Papers

Brandon F. White, Esq.
Foley Hoag LLP, Boston

§ 2.1   Introduction 2–1
§ 2.2   Verified Complaint 2–2
§ 2.3   Supporting Affidavits 2–3
§ 2.4   Motion for a Preliminary Injunction and Proposed Order 2–4
§ 2.5   Memorandum in Support of Motion for Preliminary Injunction 2–5
§ 2.6   Motion for Short Order of Notice 2–6
§ 2.7   Motion for Special Process Server 2–7
EXHIBIT 2A—Verified Complaint 2–8
EXHIBIT 2B—Motion for a Short Order of Notice 2–15
EXHIBIT 2C—Motion for Appointment of a Special Process Server 2–17

§ 2.1   INTRODUCTION

When seeking a preliminary injunction, you generally will need to prepare the following papers:

- verified complaint,

- supporting affidavits,

- motion for a preliminary injunction,

- proposed order,

- memorandum in support of the motion for a preliminary injunction,

- motion for short order of notice, and

- motion for special process server.

Practice Note
Because time is of the essence in preparing and filing the preliminary injunction papers, it is critically important to plan for the logistics involved. Do you need secretarial overtime? Is additional attorney support required? Are the important witnesses available in person or by telephone? How are you going to arrange for signatures on the affidavits? Do you have the documents to be attached as exhibits? These are just a few of the logistical issues you will need to address.

§ 2.2   VERIFIED COMPLAINT

Filing a complaint is usually required before a TRO or preliminary injunction may be obtained. Super. Ct. R. 20 ("No restraining order, injunction or other proceeding shall be ordered until the complaint is filed, unless for good cause shown."). The normal practice is to file a complaint that is verified by a person who has firsthand knowledge of the facts. If the complaint is not verified, it is essential to submit a supporting affidavit stating the facts under the penalties of perjury. *Planned Parenthood League of Mass., Inc. v. Operation Rescue*, 406 Mass. 701, 713 (1990). See **Exhibit 2A.**

Draft the verified complaint carefully. The complaint should contain not only the allegations necessary to establish your legal claims, but also a statement of facts warranting preliminary injunctive relief. Because of the importance of the verified complaint to the court's consideration of the preliminary injunction motion, you should take particular care in presenting the facts clearly and persuasively. You should resist the temptation to rely solely on "notice pleading."

The verified complaint should contain the following sections:

- an introduction briefly describing the nature of your claims,

- a section describing the parties to the dispute,

- a statement of facts,

- the various counts or legal claims, and

- a prayer for relief.

The prayer for relief should specifically describe the injunctive relief sought, including a TRO (where applicable), preliminary injunction, and permanent injunction.

Practice Note

In the rush to file the preliminary injunction papers, there is a risk that an attorney may be careless in drafting the verified complaint. Make sure you are never sloppy at this stage. In one case, a Superior Court judge vacated a preliminary injunction when it was shown, after some initial discovery, that the verified complaint and supporting affidavit contained important misstatements. *Bos. Select Grp., Inc. v. Ristaino*, 5 Mass. L. Rptr. No. 18, 414 (Mass. Super. Ct. May 3, 1996) ("The process of applying for temporary or preliminary injunctive relief demands full and complete honesty and precision.").

Judicial Commentary

Where appropriate, do not forget to include a claim for monetary damages at law. Also, keep in mind that if you do not include a jury claim, it may be deemed waived. Mass. R. Civ. P. 38(d). You should, of course, include statutory claims such as those under G.L. c. 93A and G.L. c. 21E if you have them. Lay out your claims at law in a form that does not weaken your prayers for short-term and long-term equitable relief.

§ 2.3   SUPPORTING AFFIDAVITS

If the complaint is verified, there is no requirement that additional supporting affidavits be submitted. *Alexander & Alexander, Inc. v. Danahy*, 21 Mass. App. Ct. 488, 493–94 (1986). It is, however, generally a good idea to provide the court with additional supporting affidavits, including ones from witnesses other than the plaintiff. The supporting affidavits can fill in the factual details that may be omitted from the complaint. They can be used to persuade the court that there are numerous corroborating witnesses and that the plaintiff's case is well supported. You cannot rely on facts at the preliminary hearing that are not described in the verified complaint or supporting affidavits unless they are contained in authenticated documents or deposition transcripts, or they constitute matters as to which the court can take judicial notice. *French v. Vandkjaer*, 14 Mass. App. Ct. 980, 980 (1982) (rescript).

Draft the supporting affidavits with care. All too often, the plaintiff's supporting affidavits contain false or misleading statements that can easily be attacked by the defendant. Such affidavits will not only harm your chances of obtaining a preliminary injunction, but they will also often haunt you for the rest of the litigation.

Ethics Commentary

An affidavit or verified complaint that contains incorrect information sometimes results in a complaint to bar counsel by the opposing party. If the attorney is found to have knowingly participated in a false or misleading statement, substantial public discipline will result. *See, e.g., In re McCarthy*, 9 Mass. Att'y Disc. R. 225 (1993) (presumptive one-year suspension) (and cases cited). Failure to review documents carefully that results in erroneous information being supplied to the court may result in discipline for inadequate preparation or lack of zealous representation, even if the attorney had no intent to deceive or mislead the court. *See* 11 Mass. Att'y Disc. R. 373 (1995) (careless drafting of affidavits containing misleading statements).

The information contained in each affidavit should, to the extent possible, be based on firsthand, personal knowledge. The affidavit should expressly state that it is based on the affiant's personal knowledge where that is the case, and it should describe the underlying circumstances that demonstrate this fact. An example of such a statement is the following: "I served as the defendant's supervisor for the past five years." There is, however, no inflexible rule that requires *all* of the evidence supporting a preliminary injunction to be admissible at trial. *Planned Parenthood League of Mass., Inc. v. Operation Rescue*, 406 Mass. 701, 711–12 n.9 (1990); *Brookline v. Goldstein*, 388 Mass. 443, 450 n.10 (1983). This is because facts are not finally adjudicated at the preliminary injunction stage; the court instead determines whether the plaintiff is likely to succeed on the merits.

The affiants must attest to the truthfulness of the statements. Generally, this is done by stating that the statements were made "under the penalties of perjury." G.L. c. 268, § 1A; Super. Ct. R. 15.

It is critical that the affidavit be credible. *See Farley v. Sprague*, 374 Mass. 419, 423 (1978). An affidavit that contains legalese, argument, and $10 words (or other indications that the affidavit was drafted solely by the plaintiff's attorney) is less likely to be persuasive to a court than an affidavit in the words and language of the affiant.

Practice Note

Remember that the affidavits you file with the court are a permanent record of your witnesses' testimony. They can provide a fertile basis for cross-examination. Therefore, balance the need to give the court sufficient information to win the motion with the need not to disclose your entire case.

Ethics Commentary

All too often, in a hurry to complete an affidavit or other notarized document, an attorney or someone in their office who is a notary, notarizes the signature of the client even though that person was not physically present before the notary when the document was signed. Even if the client authorized or ratified the signature and the signature is genuine, notarizing the signature of a person who was not present before the notary constitutes a violation of Mass. R. Prof. C. 8.4(c) (conduct involving a misrepresentation) and the attorney may be disciplined. *See, e.g.,* 9 Mass. Att'y Disc. R. 394 (1993). Notarization is not required so long as the statement is declared to be signed under the penalties of perjury. G.L. c. 268, § 1A. Whether notarized or not, being in a rush is no excuse for signing a client's name to an affidavit, even if it is read to the client. "One cannot sign another person's name under oath, with or without authorization." 16 Mass. Att'y Disc. R. 447 (2000).

§ 2.4   MOTION FOR A PRELIMINARY INJUNCTION AND PROPOSED ORDER

Prepare a short motion requesting that the court enter a preliminary injunction. The motion should state in summary form the grounds for the motion and refer the court to the accompanying memorandum and affidavits. *See* Mass. R. Civ. P. 7(b)(1). The motion should be styled as an "emergency" motion to fall into one of the exceptions to Super. Ct. R. 9A's usual procedure for service and filing. Super. Ct. R. 9A(e)(1).

Attach the proposed preliminary injunction to the motion. This is a key document. Pursuant to Mass. R. Civ. P. 65(d), the proposed order should be "specific in terms." The order should describe the parties who are to be enjoined and should "describe in reasonable detail, and not by reference to the complaint or other document, the act or acts sought to be restrained." The specificity requirements of Rule 65(d) are satisfied only if the enjoined party can "ascertain from the four corners of the order precisely what acts are forbidden." *Fonar Corp. v. Deccaid Servs.*, 983 F.2d 427, 430 (2d Cir. 1993) (preliminary injunction vacated where injunction was "too indefinite and ambiguous" to permit enforcement); *Sax v. Sax*, 53 Mass. App. Ct. 765, 772 (2002).

Practice Note

It is important to provide the court with a proposed order. Superior Court judges are busy and have limited secretarial resources. A carefully drafted proposed order will often expedite issuance of the desired order. In some cases, you may even consider providing the judge with proposed findings of fact, even though any facts "found" at the preliminary injunction stage remain preliminary and "are not binding on the ultimate factfinder." *Plastic Surgical Servs., P.C. v. Hall,* 1 Mass. L. Rptr. 225 (Mass. Super. Ct. Oct. 13, 1993) (citing *Packaging Indus. Grp., Inc. v. Cheney,* 380 Mass. 609, 616 (1980)). Superior Court judges typically issue such findings, although they are not required under Mass. R. Civ. P. 65.

Ethics Commentary

You should give opposing counsel a copy of any proposed order (or proposed findings of fact) so as not to run afoul of the prohibition on ex parte contact with the tribunal. *See* Mass. R. Prof. C. 3.5(a), (b).

Pursuant to Super. Ct. R. 9A(c)(3), you are presumptively entitled to a hearing; Superior Court judges almost always conduct a hearing on a motion for a preliminary injunction. Nevertheless, you should formally request a hearing in your motion. Super. Ct. R. 9A(c)(3).

§ 2.5 MEMORANDUM IN SUPPORT OF MOTION FOR PRELIMINARY INJUNCTION

The purpose of the memorandum is to explain to the court why you are entitled to a preliminary injunction. Typically, the memorandum is structured as follows:

- introduction,
- statement of facts,
- legal standard for issuance of preliminary injunction,
- argument, and
- conclusion.

The introduction concisely explains why you are entitled to preliminary injunctive relief. The statement of facts summarizes the key facts that control resolution of the dispute and weaves together the facts described in the verified complaint and supporting affidavits. Each fact contained in the memorandum should be supported by the verified complaint or supporting affidavits, and specific references to the record should be provided to the court. By the time the judge has read your statement of facts, they are probably well on the way to deciding the merits of your motion. Superior Court judges are familiar with the legal standard for issuance of a preliminary injunction, so little space should be devoted to this issue.

Judicial Commentary

Keep it simple. Lay out the relevant facts in a short paragraph if feasible. Similarly, describe the irreparable harm in another short paragraph. Do not begin your argument by stating the criteria for a preliminary injunction, as judges know them. Rather, refer to these criteria in your argument by illustrating them with facts.

The legal argument should address the factors that determine the appropriateness of a preliminary injunction, including the following:

- the plaintiff's likelihood of success on the merits,

- the irreparable harm that the plaintiff will suffer in the absence of a preliminary injunction, and

- the lack of irreparable harm to the defendant if the preliminary injunction is issued.

Where appropriate, the public interest factor should also be addressed. The conclusion should describe the specific injunctive relief sought or refer the court to the proposed order.

Pursuant to Super. Ct. R. 9A(a)(5), the memorandum should not exceed twenty double-spaced pages. Superior Court judges are generally receptive to longer memoranda on such an important motion, however, as long as counsel has made an appropriate request (by letter addressed to the session judge) to file a longer memorandum.

Technically, the memorandum should be served with the initial motion. Super. Ct. R. 9A(a)(1). This gives the defendant an opportunity to review the plaintiff's arguments and frame an appropriate response. Because of the expedited nature of a motion for a preliminary injunction, however, it is common for the plaintiff to submit its supporting memorandum at or just prior to the preliminary injunction hearing. Common courtesy and sensitivity to the particular judge's preferences on this point should be observed.

Judicial Commentary

Avoid presenting papers to the judge in open court. Consider faxing copies for the judge's review after clearing it with the clerk for the following reasons:

- Most equity matters are heard at 2:00 p.m., and the judge will probably have been in trial all morning.
- The judge may first review your filings during lunch hour.
- Many judges are uncomfortable with reading affidavits and case precedents in open court for the first time.

§ 2.6   MOTION FOR SHORT ORDER OF NOTICE

This is an ex parte motion in which you request that the court issue a short order of notice on your motion for a preliminary injunction, i.e., that the defendant be compelled to respond to your motion on an expedited basis. *See* Super. Ct. R. 9A(e)(1). The court normally will schedule a preliminary injunction hearing within four to seven days of filing the complaint and motion. See **Exhibit 2B**.

Practice Note

In the absence of such a motion, you will need to comply with the normal procedure for motions in the Superior Court under Super. Ct. R. 9A. This involves allowing the defendant ten days to serve its opposition papers and then waiting for the court to schedule a hearing. Because of the delays involved, most litigants strongly prefer the "short order of notice" method for obtaining a hearing on a preliminary injunction motion.

§ 2.7   MOTION FOR SPECIAL PROCESS SERVER

Pursuant to Mass. R. Civ. P. 4(c), the complaint ordinarily will be served by a deputy sheriff in the county where the defendant resides. Because of the delays inherent in this form of service, you should request that the court appoint a special process server to serve the complaint and other papers relating to your preliminary injunction motion. Usually, you will request that a disinterested constable be appointed; the court generally will allow the motion ex parte and as a matter of course. See **Exhibit 2C**.

EXHIBIT 2A—Verified Complaint

COMMONWEALTH OF MASSACHUSETTS

MIDDLESEX, ss.   SUPERIOR COURT
                                                  CIVIL ACTION NO.

COMPUTER SOFTWARE, INC., Plaintiff	))))
v.	))
HARRY ADAMS and KOPY SOFTWARE, INC.,	))
Defendants	))

VERIFIED COMPLAINT

NATURE OF THE ACTION

1. In this action, Plaintiff seeks injunctive relief and damages against a former employee and his new employer arising from his violation of a noncompetition agreement and his misappropriation of Plaintiff's trade secrets and other confidential business information. Plaintiff seeks a preliminary injunction to prevent the immediate and irreparable harm that will result from Defendants' disclosure and use of Plaintiff's proprietary and confidential computer programs and other business information.

PARTIES

2. Plaintiff Computer Software, Inc. ("CSI") is a corporation duly organized and existing under the laws of the Commonwealth of Massachusetts, and has a principal place of business at One Hightech Center, Waltham, Massachusetts.

3. Defendant Harry Adams ("Adams") is an individual who resides at 5 Main Street, Lexington, Massachusetts.

4. Defendant Kopy Software, Inc. ("KSI") is a corporation duly organized and existing under the laws of the Commonwealth of Massachusetts and has a principal place of business at One Corporate Place, Woburn, Massachusetts.

GENERAL ALLEGATIONS

CSI—BUSINESS BACKGROUND

5. CSI designs, programs, markets and installs computer software for use by businesses engaged in the distribution of products. CSI's proprietary and confidential software includes computer programs for inventory management, sales order management, financial management and other business functions. CSI's software includes modules for inventory control, warehouse management, sales analysis, purchasing and receiving, accounts payable, accounts receivable and general ledger.

6. CSI was incorporated in 1995 and presently employs over 350 employees in four offices in the United States. CSI's offices are located in Waltham, Massachusetts; Palo Alto, California; Atlanta, Georgia; and Phoenix, Arizona. In 2005, CSI's sales revenues were in excess of $200 million.

7. CSI's proprietary and confidential software is marketed and licensed to users throughout the United States. CSI's software is used by a variety of industries, including wholesale and retail distributors of automotive parts, electronic equipment and supplies, industrial chemicals, pharmaceuticals, food manufacturers and distributors, and consumer goods.

KSI—BUSINESS BACKGROUND

8. KSI also designs, programs, markets and installs computer software for use by businesses engaged in the distribution of products. Upon information and belief, KSI was incorporated in July 2008 and presently employs approximately 50 employees.

9. KSI is one of CSI's principal competitors in the business software market. Like CSI, KSI markets computer programs for inventory management, sales order management, financial management and other business functions. Like CSI, KSI software operates on Digital's VAX hardware and utilizes Digital's VMS operating system. Like CSI, KSI has offices in the Boston area and in Palo Alto, and markets its software throughout the United States. Like CSI, KSI markets its software to large companies with annual revenues exceeding $500 million. As a result, KSI and CSI frequently compete for many of the same customers.

CSI'S TRADE SECRETS AND CONFIDENTIAL INFORMATION

10. Because of the competitive nature of the business software industry, companies such as CSI must protect their trade secrets and confidential business information. This proprietary and confidential information includes, for example: CSI's source and object code for its computer software; many of the operational and functional features and limitations of its computer software; the manner in which the computer software is installed at a customer's site; the prices, terms and conditions of CSI's contracts with its customers; its pricing and price lists; and its financial information.

11. CSI takes numerous precautions to protect its trade secrets and confidential business information. CSI limits dissemination of such information to those with a need to know; takes physical security measures; requires its customers to sign

nondisclosure agreements, and requires its employees, such as Adams, to sign employment agreements that contain noncompetition and nondisclosure provisions.

CSI'S CUSTOMER GOODWILL

12. The development and enhancement of customer goodwill is a critical factor in ensuring CSI's success. Over the years and at great expense, CSI has established and cultivated relationships with hundreds of customers located throughout the United States.

13. CSI conducts repeat business with many of its customers by selling additional software modules and additional products and services to them.

EMPLOYMENT AND RESIGNATION OF ADAMS

14. On January 1, 2003, Adams commenced his employment with CSI as a Software Programmer. As a Software Programmer, Adams's duties included: learning the details of CSI's proprietary and confidential software, programming and debugging the software, assisting in making proposals to potential customers, formulating test data for product demonstrations, making sales presentations to potential customers, and conducting training classes for customers.

15. On January 1, 2003, Adams signed an Employment Agreement with CSI. The Agreement provided, inter alia, that Adams would not compete for a one-year period after his termination and that he would not furnish any of CSI's confidential information to anyone at any time. In pertinent part, the Agreement states as follows:

> The Employee agrees that during his employment by the Company, and for a period of one year thereafter, he will not become employed by or act on behalf of any other person, corporation or entity that is engaged in any business or activity similar to or directly or indirectly competitive with that of the Company.

* * *

> The Employee agrees during his employment by Company, and thereafter, to hold in confidence and not to disclose any of the Confidential Information to anyone, or utilize any of the Confidential Information for any purpose, except in the course of the Employee's work for Company.

A true and correct copy of the Agreement signed by Adams is attached hereto as Exhibit A, and is incorporated by reference.

16. The Agreement further provides that Adams acknowledges that CSI will provide him with access to confidential information during the course of his employment, and that CSI will be entitled to injunctive relief to enforce the terms of the Agreement. In pertinent part, the Agreement states as follows:

The Employee acknowledges that the Company will, in reliance upon this agreement, provide Employee access to confidential data, and that the provisions of this agreement are reasonably necessary to protect the Company's legitimate interests.

* * *

Because of the unique nature of the Confidential Information, the Employee understands and agrees that the Company will suffer irreparable harm in the event that the Employee fails to comply with the obligations of this Agreement, and that monetary damages will be inadequate to compensate Company for such breach. Accordingly, the Employee agrees that the Company will, in addition to any other remedies available to it at law or in equity, be entitled to injunctive relief to enforce the terms of this Agreement.

17. Because of the complexity of CSI's proprietary and confidential software, Adams spent literally hundreds of hours mastering the operational and functional features and limitations of the software. In addition, Adams used and became familiar with other CSI confidential information, including the manner in which the computer software is installed at a customer's site; the prices, terms and conditions of CSI's contracts with customers; its pricing and price lists; and its financial information. Adams also had contacts with and became familiar with certain of CSI's customers.

18. On October 4, 2014, after almost twelve years' service with CSI, Adams voluntarily resigned his position as Software Programmer for CSI. Adams failed and refused to tell CSI who his new employer would be.

19. CSI subsequently learned that Adams commenced employment with KSI as a software programmer on or about October 7, 2014.

20. On October 15, 2014, CSI sent a letter to Adams reminding him of his obligations not to compete with CSI for a period of one year, and notifying him that CSI considered his employment with KSI to be in breach of his agreement. A true and correct copy of the letter is attached hereto as Exhibit B, and is incorporated by reference.

21. On October 15, 2014, CSI sent a letter to KSI stating that CSI understood that Adams had accepted a position with KSI, and that CSI considered Adams's employment with KSI to be in breach of his agreement. A true and correct copy of the letter is attached hereto as Exhibit C, and is incorporated by reference.

22. Notwithstanding the express terms of the Agreement and the foregoing letters, Adams has remained in the employ of KSI in breach of his obligations to CSI.

COUNT I
BREACH OF CONTRACT—ADAMS

23. CSI realleges and incorporates by reference its allegations in Paragraphs 1–22, above.

24. CSI has fully performed any obligations to Adams under the parties' Agreement.

25. Adams has failed to perform his obligations to CSI under the parties' Agreement.

26. Adams's breach of the Agreement presents an immediate threat of irreparable harm to CSI. In addition, Adams has caused CSI damages in an amount to be determined at trial.

COUNT II
INTERFERENCE WITH CONTRACTUAL RELATIONS—KSI

27. CSI realleges and incorporates by reference its allegations in Paragraphs 1–26, above.

28. KSI knew, or should have known, that Adams had a preexisting contract with CSI.

29. Despite said knowledge, KSI interfered with said contract.

30. Said interference by KSI was intentional, malicious, and without lawful justification.

31. As a direct result thereof, Adams has breached his contract with CSI, causing damages to CSI.

COUNT III
MISAPPROPRIATION OF TRADE SECRETS AND
CONFIDENTIAL INFORMATION—ADAMS AND KSI

32. CSI realleges and incorporates by reference its allegations in Paragraphs 1–31, above.

33. Upon information and belief, Adams has or will disclose to KSI or others certain of CSI's trade secrets and confidential information.

34. Upon information and belief, Adams has or will use during the course of his employment by KSI certain of CSI's trade secrets and confidential information.

35. The disclosure and use of such information by the Defendants constitute a misappropriation of trade secrets and confidential information in violation of common law and of G.L. c. 93, §§ 42 and 42A.

36. CSI will suffer substantial, immediate and irreparable harm and damages unless Defendants are enjoined from disclosing and using such trade secrets and confidential business information. In addition, Defendants have or will cause CSI damages in an amount to be determined at trial. Such damages include, without limitation, CSI's lost profits and Defendants' wrongful profits derived by said unauthorized disclosure or use.

COUNT IV

VIOLATIONS OF G.L. C. 93A—ADAMS AND KSI

37. CSI realleges and incorporates by reference its allegations in Paragraphs 1–36, above.

38. CSI is a "person" and engages in "trade or commerce" within the meaning of G.L. c. 93A, § 1.

39. The Defendants are "persons" and engage in "trade or commerce" within the meaning of G.L. c. 93A, § 1.

40. The Defendants' practices, as set forth above, constitute willful and knowing violations of G.L. c. 93A.

41. As a direct result thereof, CSI will suffer substantial, immediate and irreparable harm and damages unless Defendants are enjoined from their unlawful activity. In addition, Defendants owe CSI treble damages in an amount to be determined at trial.

RELIEF

WHEREFORE, Plaintiff CSI prays that this Court:

1. Issue its Summons and Order of Notice that Defendants answer this Verified Complaint and appear for a hearing on CSI's Motion for a Preliminary Injunction at 2:00 p.m. on October 24, 2014.

2. Appoint a person specially to serve process.

3. After a hearing, issue a preliminary injunction enjoining and restraining Defendants and their agents, servants, employees and attorneys from (a) causing or allowing Adams to work for or on behalf of KSI prior to October 1, 2015, and (b) disclosing or using any of CSI's trade secrets or confidential business information, including, without limitation: CSI's source and object code for its computer software; information regarding the operational and functional features and limitations of CSI's computer software; the manner in which CSI's computer software is installed at a customer's site; the prices, terms and conditions of CSI's contracts with its customers; CSI's pricing and price lists; and CSI's financial information.

4. After trial, enter a permanent injunction in the form as set out in Paragraph 3, above, and award CSI its damages, attorneys' fees, costs and interest pursuant to Counts I through IV of the Complaint. CSI requests that damages pursuant to Counts

III and IV be doubled or trebled pursuant to G.L. c. 93, § 42 and G.L. c. 93A, § 11, respectively.

5. Award CSI such other relief as the Court may deem just and proper.

COMPUTER SOFTWARE, INC.
By its Attorneys,

_____
Attorney(s) (BBO No. XXXXXX)
Firm Name
Address
Phone

Dated:

VERIFICATION

I, SAMUEL GOODRIGHT, hereby depose and state as follows:

1. I am President and Chief Executive Officer of Computer Software, Inc., the Plaintiff in the above-captioned case.

2. I have read the Verified Complaint filed herein and, knowing the contents thereof, have found that the allegations of fact set forth therein are based on my own personal knowledge and are true, except as to those allegations based on information and belief which I believe to be true.

Signed under the penalties of perjury on this _____ day of October, 20__.

_____
Samuel Goodright

CERTIFICATE OF SERVICE

I hereby certify that the above document is being served within the time required by Superior Court Standing Order No. No. 1-88 except as modified by the Session Judge or by the Regional Administrative Justice. I further certify that I served a true copy of this document upon the attorney of record for each party by hand/mail on [date].

_____

EXHIBIT 2B—Motion for a Short Order of Notice

COMMONWEALTH OF MASSACHUSETTS

MIDDLESEX, ss.   SUPERIOR COURT
                                                                  CIVIL ACTION NO.

[NAME], Plaintiff	))))
v.	))
[NAME], Defendants	))))

MOTION FOR A SHORT ORDER OF NOTICE

Pursuant to Superior Court Rule 9A(e)(1), the Plaintiff _____ moves that the Court issue a Summons and Order of Notice that Defendants answer the Verified Complaint and appear for a hearing on Plaintiff's Motion for a Preliminary Injunction at 2:00 p.m. on October 24, 20__. In support of this Motion, Plaintiff states that it is seeking a preliminary injunction to prevent a former employee and his new employer from violating the former employee's one-year noncompete Agreement, and to prevent the former employee and his new employer from improperly using or disclosing Plaintiff's trade secrets and confidential business information. An expedited hearing is required to prevent irreparable harm to Plaintiff. In further support of this Motion, Plaintiff relies on its Verified Complaint.

Plaintiff
By its Attorneys,

Attorney(s) (BBO No. XXXXXX)
Firm Name
Address
Phone

Dated:

CERTIFICATE OF SERVICE

I hereby certify that the above document is being served within the time required by Superior Court Standing Order No. No. 1-88 except as modified by the Session Judge or by the Regional Administrative Justice. I further certify that I served a true copy of this document upon the attorney of record for each party by hand/mail on [date].

_____

EXHIBIT 2C—Motion for Appointment of a Special Process Server

COMMONWEALTH OF MASSACHUSETTS

MIDDLESEX, ss.   SUPERIOR COURT
                                                          CIVIL ACTION NO.

[NAME],
         Plaintiff
 	
v.
 	
[NAME],
         Defendants
	)
	)
	)
	)
	)
	)
	)
	)
	)
	)

MOTION FOR APPOINTMENT OF A SPECIAL PROCESS SERVER

     Pursuant to Mass. R. Civ. P. 4(c), Plaintiff _____ hereby moves for an order appointing Constable Bernard Witten, or his employees or agents, as special process server in the above-captioned action. The person to be appointed special process server is experienced in the service of process, is 18 years of age or older, and is not a party to this action.

                                     Plaintiff
                                     By its Attorneys,

                                   _____
                                   Attorney(s) (BBO No. XXXXXX)
                                   Firm Name
                                   Address
                                   Phone

Dated:

CERTIFICATE OF SERVICE

     I hereby certify that the above document is being served within the time required by Superior Court Standing Order No. No. 1-88 except as modified by the Session Judge or by the Regional Administrative Justice. I further certify that I served a true copy of this document upon the attorney of record for each party by hand/mail on [date].

_____

CHAPTER 3

Filing the Injunction Papers

Brandon F. White, Esq.
Foley Hoag LLP, Boston

§ 3.1 THE FILING PROCESS

After the injunction papers are prepared and the verified complaint and affidavits are signed by the witnesses, you should commence the lawsuit by filing the papers with the court. In addition to the papers described above, there are two more things you will need to bring to court: the civil action cover sheet and the filing fee.

The precise procedure may vary slightly from court to court, but the procedure in Middlesex Superior Court, outlined below, is typical.

- Go to the civil clerk's office and file the papers. Inform the clerk that you are seeking a preliminary injunction and that you would like the court to approve your motion for a short order of notice and motion for a special process server.

- After the papers have been assigned a civil action number, you will be given the file and told to go to the session of the judge who has been assigned the case.

- Go to the courtroom and see the courtroom clerk. Explain that you are seeking a short order of notice and appointment of a special process server in connection with a preliminary injunction motion.

Judicial Commentary
Clerks, especially courtroom clerks, are a wealth of information as to the procedures and sensitivities of the judges they work with. Treat clerks as professionals and you will reap rewards.

- The clerk usually will present the papers to the judge in their chambers and will emerge with the notations that both motions (the short order of notice and appointment of a special process server) have been "allowed." Sometimes, however, you will appear before the judge and will need to explain briefly why the two motions should be allowed. These motions are routinely granted in the Superior Court.

- You will then go to the equity clerk, who will draft a summons and short order of notice.

Practice Note
Barnstable, Middlesex, Suffolk, and Worcester Superior Courts allow for electronic filing for civil contract and business cases, equitable remedies,

real property, actions involving state and municipality, administrative civil actions, miscellaneous civil actions, torts, and, in Suffolk only, business litigation. Depending on where you file your case, this might also be an option.

- After receiving the summons and short order of notice, you will arrange for prompt service on the defendant by the special process server. You will need to provide to the special process server a copy of the allowed motion appointing the process server, along with the other papers to be served upon the defendant.

Practice Note

Do not wait until the very end of the day to attempt to accomplish all of this. Generally, if you initiate the process by 3:00 p.m., you will be able to complete all of the above steps by the time the court closes for the day.

CHAPTER 4

Opposing a Motion for a Preliminary Injunction

Brandon F. White, Esq.
Foley Hoag LLP, Boston

§ 4.1   Initial Considerations 4–1

§ 4.2   Standstill Agreement 4–3

§ 4.3   Opposition Affidavits.. 4–3

§ 4.4   Opposition Memorandum.. 4–4

EXHIBIT 4A—Standstill Agreement.. 4–5

§ 4.1   INITIAL CONSIDERATIONS

Usually, you will receive a call from an upset and anxious client who explains that they have just been served with a complaint and an order scheduling a preliminary injunction hearing within a few days. This is no time to panic. Initially, you should take the following steps.

First, you should obtain and carefully review all of the court papers and meet with your client. Your initial objective is to understand the underlying facts and the claims being made by the plaintiff. You should review each paragraph of the verified complaint and supporting affidavits to separate fact from fiction.

Judicial Commentary
Immediately identify each potential witness with whom you may want to speak and be sure that they remain available to meet or talk with you on short notice.

Ethics Commentary
In dealing with unrepresented potential witnesses, be cognizant of the restrictions of Mass. R. Prof. C. 4.3, entitled "dealing with unrepresented persons."

Second, you should consider the merits of the case and any available defenses. Has the plaintiff stated valid claims? Can the plaintiff satisfy the requirements for a preliminary injunction?

Third, you should develop your strategy for dealing with the preliminary injunction motion. There are a variety of possible responses, including the following:

- contact opposing counsel and attempt a settlement;

- contact opposing counsel and request a postponement of the hearing to allow you and your client an adequate opportunity to prepare;

- contact opposing counsel and arrange for a "standstill agreement" to allow you and your client an adequate opportunity to prepare;

- contact opposing counsel and arrange for an interim agreement that provides a modicum of relief, but is neither catastrophic nor severely prejudicial to the parties; or

- contact opposing counsel, introduce yourself, request that any further papers be copied to you, and prepare your opposition to the motion for a preliminary injunction.

Practice Note

Whether you represent the plaintiff or the defendant, it is usually a good idea to speak with opposing counsel *before* the preliminary injunction hearing. Many Superior Court judges will inquire as to what efforts the parties have made to resolve the dispute informally and will not be impressed when counsel shrug their shoulders and explain that they have not even spoken to each other.

Judicial Commentary

It cannot hurt to represent that you have taken the lead in trying to resolve the matter informally and, failing that, you have suggested early mediation.

Ethics Commentary

If the opposing party is unrepresented, any effort at informal resolution must proceed with extreme caution. Rule 4.3(b) of the Massachusetts Rules of Professional Conduct prohibits a lawyer from giving advice to a person whose interests are likely to be adverse to the client's, other than the advice to seek counsel. Rule 4.3(a) of the Massachusetts Rules of Professional Conduct requires a lawyer dealing with an unrepresented person to refrain from holding themselves out as disinterested and, if the person evinces a misunderstanding of the lawyer's role in the matter, to make reasonable efforts to correct the misunderstanding.

Generally, but not always, you will need additional time to prepare for the preliminary injunction hearing. Typically, the plaintiff has had at least several days to prepare its papers. Often, four to seven days is insufficient time to respond. Superior Court judges are generally sympathetic to a defendant's plea for more time, although they may condition such additional time on providing the plaintiff with some interim relief so that no irreparable harm occurs prior to the hearing.

Judicial Commentary

Try to avoid a situation where you file an opposition in court right before the hearing. It places the judge in a very uncomfortable position to have a stack of unread papers on the bench that are important to the resolution of the motion being heard.

§ 4.2   STANDSTILL AGREEMENT

A standstill agreement, as the name implies, is an agreement whereby the parties agree that they will maintain the status quo until the postponed hearing date. A standstill agreement affords the defendant some "breathing room" to prepare its affidavits and opposition memorandum and to consider its case strategy. A standstill agreement, however, might require the defendant in effect to grant the plaintiff a TRO for a short period of time, and thereby provide the plaintiff with at least some short-term relief. See **Exhibit 4A**.

Practice Note
In drafting a standstill agreement, the plaintiff should include language that the agreement continues until the judge renders a decision on the motion. Otherwise, there will be a "gap" between the hearing date and the date of the judge's decision—a period that can range from a day to a month or more. The plaintiff also may want to specify the exact dates that the defendant must serve its affidavits and opposition memorandum to avoid receiving all of these documents at the last minute on the day of the hearing. The defendant should include language in the standstill agreement that makes it clear that the defendant is not waiving any of its rights or conceding in any way that the plaintiff is entitled to a preliminary injunction.

§ 4.3   OPPOSITION AFFIDAVITS

The number and quality of the defendant's opposition affidavits may well determine the outcome of the preliminary injunction motion. In drafting the opposition affidavits, look to the following three principal objectives for guidance:

- expose any false or misleading "facts" in the plaintiff's verified complaint and supporting affidavits,

- tell your side of the story in a compelling way, and

- persuade the judge that the equities (including the "balance of harms" and the plaintiff's "unclean hands") require denial of the motion.

Like the plaintiff's affidavits, the opposition affidavits, to the extent possible, should be based on personal knowledge, and they should be carefully drafted to ensure that they are accurate and complete. If the facts are in sharp dispute, providing numerous affiants who attest to your side of the story will be helpful in persuading the judge that either your version is accurate or, at worst, there are substantial disputed facts and therefore a preliminary injunction is inappropriate. *A-Copy, Inc. v. Michaelson*, 599 F.2d 450, 451 (1st Cir. 1978) ("a court should be reluctant to grant preliminary relief if there is a close factual dispute which could go either way at the trial on the merits").

Pursuant to Mass. R. Civ. P. 6(c), "opposing affidavits may be served not later than 1 day before the hearing, unless the court permits them to be served at some other time." It is good practice, therefore, to serve any opposition affidavits at least one day before the scheduled hearing. There are circumstances, however, when compliance with this rule is impractical. Most Superior Court judges will allow late-filed affidavits if there is a reasonable basis for the delay.

Practice Note

You should consider a motion to strike affidavits that are not based on firsthand, personal knowledge or are otherwise improper, even though the rules of evidence are applied less strictly than at trial. If the motion to strike is not made, the court may be more reluctant to discount hearsay statements included in your opponent's affidavits.

§ 4.4   OPPOSITION MEMORANDUM

The defendant's memorandum should synthesize the facts, based on the affidavits, and describe to the court the legal bases for denying the motion. Assuming that a short order of notice has been issued and that the preliminary injunction hearing is conducted on short notice, the opposition memorandum is generally served at the hearing. If this is done, it is considered good practice to serve the memorandum on opposing counsel immediately upon arrival in court, rather than waiting until the actual argument.

Be thorough in searching for similar cases in which injunctions have been denied. Although every case is unique, and preliminary injunction rulings are discretionary, you may find a body of law, or a trend, favoring your position, which can tip the scales in your favor.

The defendant should not assume that the judge will automatically require an injunction bond, and should take this opportunity to request one. If no injunction bond is required, the defendant will not be able to recover damages arising from a wrongfully issued injunction. *Thayer Co. v. Binnall*, 326 Mass. 467, 480 (1950).

Judicial Commentary

Even if you are served late, avoid filing affidavits, memoranda, and authorities in open court at the hearing. Use a fax machine and call the clerk. No judge wants to be presented with a mound of paper to read in open court.

Ethics Commentary

In drafting any legal memorandum, counsel should keep in mind the requirement of Mass. R. Prof. C. 3.3(a)(3), which requires a lawyer to disclose to the court any controlling legal authority directly adverse to their client's position that has not been disclosed by opposing counsel.

EXHIBIT 4A—Standstill Agreement

COMMONWEALTH OF MASSACHUSETTS

MIDDLESEX, ss.   SUPERIOR COURT
                                                           CIVIL ACTION NO.

COMPUTER SOFTWARE, INC.,	)
Plaintiff	)
	)
v.	)
	)
HARRY ADAMS and KOPY SOFTWARE, INC.,	)
	)
Defendants	)
	)

STANDSTILL AGREEMENT

Plaintiff Computer Software, Inc. ("CSI") and Defendants Harry Adams ("Adams") and Kopy Software, Inc. ("KSI") hereby stipulate and agree as follows:

1. The hearing on CSI's motion for a preliminary injunction has been continued to November 1, 2014 at 2:00 p.m.

2. Until further order of the Court, Defendants shall not (a) cause or allow Adams to work for or on behalf of KSI; and (b) disclose or use any of CSI's trade secrets or confidential business information except as may be necessary to defend this litigation, and, in this event, only pursuant to the terms of a protective order agreed to by the parties or otherwise entered by the Court.

3. The parties will not initiate or conduct any discovery prior to the hearing scheduled for November 1, 2014.

4. CSI will file its Memorandum in Support of Its Motion for a Preliminary Injunction on or before October 25, 2014. CSI will serve a copy of the Memorandum upon Defendants' counsel by hand on or before October 25, 2014.

5. Defendants will serve by hand copies of all of their opposition papers (including affidavits and memoranda) upon CSI's counsel on or before 12:00 p.m. on October 30, 2014.

6. By entering into this Standstill Agreement, Defendants do not waive, and expressly reserve, all of their rights and defenses.

COMPUTER SOFTWARE, INC.   HARRY ADAMS and KOPY
                                 SOFTWARE, INC.
By its Attorneys,   By their Attorneys,

_____   _____
Attorney(s) (BBO No. XXXXXX)   Attorney(s) (BBO No. XXXXXX)
Firm Name   Firm Name
Address   Address
Phone   Phone

Dated: _____

APPROVED BY THE COURT:

Dated: _____   _____
                                 (_____, J.)

CHAPTER 5

Preliminary Injunction Hearing

Brandon F. White, Esq.
Foley Hoag LLP, Boston

§ 5.1   **Preparing for the Hearing**.. **5–1**
    § 5.1.1   Arrange to Have Your Client Present.................................... 5–1
    § 5.1.2   Arrive Early at the Court... 5–2
    § 5.1.3   Consider the Need to File Rebuttal Affidavits
                or a Supplemental Memorandum 5–2
    § 5.1.4   Consider How You Are Going to Handle the Security
                Issue 5–2
    § 5.1.5   Bring to Court Extra Copies of All of the Filed Papers.......... 5–3
    § 5.1.6   Prepare Your Oral Argument 5–3

§ 5.1   PREPARING FOR THE HEARING

Whether you represent the plaintiff or the defendant, you should prepare carefully for the oral argument and take the following steps.

Judicial Commentary
Look at where you appear in the court's session calendar. Estimate for the clerk how long your matter will take. Be agreeable to allowing others with shorter matters to be heard first, even though injunctions may be scheduled first.

§ 5.1.1   Arrange to Have Your Client Present

This demonstrates to the court that this is an important motion and that your client cares about the outcome. It also allows you to deal intelligently with any last-minute affidavits that may be filed by opposing counsel. If your client is not present at the hearing, it will be difficult or impossible to deal with factual allegations made in such last-minute affidavits.

Judicial Commentary
Your client will not go unnoticed by the judge. Make sure that the client dresses and acts appropriately. Prepare the client for the possibility of questions from you or the judge.

Practice Note
Superior Court judges rarely allow evidentiary hearings on preliminary injunction motions. Instead, Superior Court judges generally decide preliminary injunction motions based on the papers filed by the parties and the

oral arguments of counsel. If there is a key disputed issue of material fact, however, you may want to request a limited evidentiary hearing in your motion and discuss the issue with the court clerk prior to the hearing. One of the advantages of bringing your client to the hearing is that it allows you to offer oral testimony if it becomes necessary.

§ 5.1.2   Arrive Early at the Court

This will provide you and your client with an opportunity to review the inevitable flurry of papers filed by your opponent. Do not be shy. Upon your arrival in court, ask your opposing counsel whether they are planning on filing any additional documents with the court. If so, ask for them and review them as time permits while waiting for your case to be called.

§ 5.1.3   Consider the Need to File Rebuttal Affidavits or a Supplemental Memorandum

The last-minute papers filed by opposing counsel may make it important for you to file supplemental affidavits to rebut specific factual allegations not addressed in your initial affidavits. It may also be necessary to file a supplemental memorandum to deal with unanticipated legal issues. Most Superior Court judges will not be enthusiastic about receiving additional papers. If it is important to provide the judge with additional information, however, you should make sure that you request the opportunity. Be prepared to file any additional documents promptly, i.e., within a day or two of the hearing.

Judicial Commentary
If the other side presents affidavits at the hearing, consider whether you need to request a short period in which to respond with your own affidavits.

§ 5.1.4   Consider How You Are Going to Handle the Security Issue

As noted above, Mass. R. Civ. P. 65(c) generally requires that the court order some form of security as a condition of entering the preliminary injunction. As a practical matter, many Superior Court judges—as well as many practitioners—give short shrift to this requirement. Nevertheless, whether you represent the plaintiff or the defendant, you should carefully consider your position on this important issue.

Practice Note
Sometimes defense counsel are reluctant to raise the issue of security because they are concerned that it may indicate to the court that their case is weak or that they expect to lose. In many cases, it may make sense not to devote time to this issue at the oral argument. If you are opposing the entry of a preliminary injunction, however, you should, at a minimum, devote a short section of your memorandum to the issue of security. This way, you will remind the court of the issue and will not have waived your right to security.

Ethics Commentary

Bonds are rarely, if ever, required if the plaintiff seeks an injunction against the government. *See, e.g., Silva v. Romney*, 342 F. Supp. 783 (D. Mass. 1972). Likewise, bonds are not required of the government when it obtains a preliminary injunction. Mass. R. Civ. P. 65(c). Trial counsel should research special circumstances, such as a public entity as a party, so as not to run afoul of Mass. R. Prof. C. 3.1 (generally prohibiting the advance of a claim that is unwarranted under existing law).

§ 5.1.5   Bring to Court Extra Copies of All of the Filed Papers

Because of the expedited nature of the process and possible delays in the court clerk's filing or transferring papers, the judge sometimes will not have critical documents.

§ 5.1.6   Prepare Your Oral Argument

Because of the equitable and discretionary nature of a preliminary injunction, the oral argument is often critical in determining the outcome. You should be passionate but not overbearing, and explain clearly and succinctly why your client should prevail.

Ethics Commentary

Counsel should not end oral advocacy if there is any likelihood that the court is proceeding on a mistaken assumption. In *In re Mahlowitz*, 1 Mass. Att'y Disc. R. 189 (1979), a lawyer was publicly censured for failing to correct the court's erroneous belief that it had entered an order restraining his client, a husband, from selling property that the wife sought to attach as security in a contempt proceeding for support. The lawyer then assisted his client in selling the property. Although the information concerning the existence of the temporary order arguably was available to opposing counsel, the lawyer was required to reveal the information in order to prevent fraud upon the court, even though the information was prejudicial to his client. It is likely that similar facts would warrant more substantial discipline by current standards. *See In re Griffith*, 440 Mass. 500 (2003).

Be responsive to the judge's questions and view them as opportunities to respond to issues that may be troubling the judge. Be flexible. If you are representing the plaintiff and it appears that the judge is unwilling to grant the full injunction requested, explain alternatives to the judge that provide your client with at least some relief.

Practice Note

Before the oral argument, consider what alternatives to the requested injunction might be acceptable to your client, and discuss them with your client. This way, you will be prepared if the issue arises during the argument, and you will not be forced into an "all or nothing" approach.

Judicial Commentary

Try to make the judge feel positive about ruling in your favor. Judges like to resolve matters, if possible, with a minimum of harm to the losing party.

Ethics Commentary

Reasonable client communication is one of the hallmarks of the post-1998 rules of professional conduct. Rule 1.4(a) of the Massachusetts Rules of Professional Conduct specifically requires a lawyer to "keep a client reasonably informed about the status of a matter." Comment [1] provides that a lawyer should ensure that a client's decisions are made only after the client has been informed of relevant considerations. Thus, a client should be informed of the discretionary nature of equitable relief and the possibility—if not the likelihood—that the court will explore options and alternatives. Also, both counsel should have clear instructions from their clients regarding the acceptance of options. *See* Mass. R. Prof. C. 1.2(a) (lawyer is generally bound by client's instructions and directions). This is another reason why it is desirable, if not imperative, that the client attend the motion session.

CHAPTER 6

After the Hearing

Brandon F. White, Esq.
Foley Hoag LLP, Boston

§ 6.1   What to Do Prior to the Court's Decision... 6–1

§ 6.2   What to Do if the Preliminary Injunction Is Allowed 6–1

§ 6.3   Appealing the Grant or Denial of a Preliminary Injunction.............. 6–2

§ 6.4   Enforcement of a Preliminary Injunction 6–3

§ 6.1   WHAT TO DO PRIOR TO THE COURT'S DECISION

Most Superior Court judges decide preliminary injunction motions promptly—within a matter of days or a week of the hearing. If you represent the defendant and there is no TRO or standstill agreement in place, the question often arises: What should the defendant do prior to the decision?

There is no easy answer to this question; its resolution often hinges on how risk-averse your client is. Often, based on the judge's statements or questions at the hearing, there is little doubt as to how the judge is going to rule, and you can advise your client accordingly. Sometimes, though, the judge may sit sphinxlike throughout the hearing and offer little guidance as to the expected ruling. In some instances, a cautious defendant may want to stay its hand pending a ruling. In others, a more aggressive defendant may want to continue with the conduct in question.

Judicial Commentary
Keep in touch with the clerk. Show interest, but do not be a pest. You may want to ask the clerk how you can best stay in touch with them.

§ 6.2   WHAT TO DO IF THE PRELIMINARY INJUNCTION IS ALLOWED

If the court enters a preliminary injunction, there are generally two immediate steps that must be taken by the plaintiff. First, the plaintiff must serve the order on the defendant, preferably in hand. The appointment of a special process server is generally the most efficient way to effect service. Second, the plaintiff may need to obtain an injunction bond. *See* Mass. R. Civ. P. 65(c). Often, a bond can be obtained from the plaintiff's liability insurance company; if not, there are brokers who specialize in bonds for judicial proceedings. Often, the bond must be collateralized with a certificate of deposit in the full penal sum.

If you represent the defendant, you should discuss the terms of the injunction with your client and explain the importance of full, immediate compliance. Discuss how your client plans to comply with the injunction. Explain to your client that they may be found in civil or criminal contempt for failure to comply with an injunction. See § 6.4, Enforcement of a Preliminary Injunction, below.

Judicial Commentary
Although most judges are reluctant to exercise their contempt powers, they may have few alternatives.

Ethics Commentary
Although a lawyer may properly advise their client of the consequences of noncompliance, a lawyer may not "assist" or participate in any disregard or circumvention of a court-imposed obligation. *See* Mass. R. Prof. C. 3.3(a)(2), 3.4(c). Any attorney faced with a client that is disregarding a court order should seek assistance from the Office of Bar Counsel, the Massachusetts Bar Association Committee of Professional Ethics, or private counsel.

§ 6.3   APPEALING THE GRANT OR DENIAL OF A PRELIMINARY INJUNCTION

If your client is dissatisfied with the decision in the Superior Court, you have two principal appellate routes:

- an appeal to the single justice pursuant to G.L. c. 231, § 118, ¶ 1; or

- an appeal to the full Appeals Court pursuant to G.L. c. 231, § 118, ¶ 2.

There are advantages and disadvantages to both modes of appeal, although a litigant may elect to pursue both at the same time. *See Helmes v. Commonwealth*, 406 Mass. 873, 874 (1990). Neither form of appeal suspends execution of the Superior Court's order. G.L. c. 231, § 118.

Pursuant to G.L. c. 231, § 118, ¶ 1, you may seek *discretionary* review before the single justice of the Appeals Court. The single justice may do any of three things:

- decide that interlocutory appellate review is not warranted;

- decide that the matter should be referred to the full bench; or

- decide that the decision of the Superior Court should be affirmed, reversed, or modified.

The appeal to the single justice must be filed within thirty days after the order by the Superior Court. Generally, the single justice will promptly consider and rule upon such an appeal. Because of the discretionary nature of preliminary injunctions, single justices do not routinely overturn these rulings. *Edwin R. Sage Co. v. Foley*, 12 Mass. App. Ct. 20, 23 (1981). Nevertheless, the single justice "morning after" motion sessions are popular with litigants, if not the judges, and you should consider such an appeal if you have a compelling case. If the judge indicates that an injunction is to issue and you are inclined to seek appellate review, you might want to ask the judge to stay the injunction for a specific period or until the resolution of the appeal. Such relief is purely discretionary and you may well be unsuccessful.

Pursuant to G.L. c. 231, § 118, ¶ 2, you may seek review as of right before the Appeals Court. The appeal must be filed within thirty days of the Superior Court's order. The major disadvantage of this appellate procedure is that it is normally not expedited. *Demoulas Super Mkts., Inc. v. Peter's Mkt. Basket*, 5 Mass. App. Ct. 750, 753–54 (1977). As a result, if the preliminary injunction motion was denied by the Superior Court, the injunctive remedy will often be moot by the time regular appellate review occurs.

Judicial Commentary

Although our appellate courts have the reputation for being activist, single justices tend to uphold motion judges with frequency.

The Superior Court's decision granting or denying a preliminary injunction will not be reversed except for abuse of discretion, wherein the appellate court will decide "whether the judge applied proper legal standards and whether there was reasonable support for his evaluation of factual questions." *Commonwealth v. Fremont Inv. & Loan*, 452 Mass. 733, 741 (2008). Under this standard, the judge's rulings of law "will be reversed if incorrect." *Packaging Indus. Grp., Inc. v. Cheney*, 380 Mass. at 616. The judge's preliminary findings of fact will be given deference and, if live testimony is heard, the judge's credibility determinations will not be disturbed. *Packaging Indus. Grp., Inc. v. Cheney*, 380 Mass. at 616. If the order is based on documentary evidence alone—including affidavits—the reviewing court "may draw [its] own conclusions from the record." *Packaging Indus. Grp., Inc. v. Cheney*, 380 Mass. at 616; *see also Loyal Order of Moose, Inc. v. Bd. of Health of Yarmouth*, 439 Mass. 597, 602–04 (2003) (reversing denial of preliminary injunction and directing that Board of Health be enjoined from enforcing smoking ban because record showed lodge's social quarters were private rather than public).

§ 6.4 ENFORCEMENT OF A PRELIMINARY INJUNCTION

Violation of a preliminary injunction is a contempt of court; penalties can be severe. If the defendant violates a preliminary injunction, the plaintiff has two remedies: civil enforcement or criminal enforcement.

Judicial Commentary

Judges know that such proceedings are often unpleasant and contentious, and it is not uncommon for one or more interested parties to stretch the truth. Resolving the issue may amount to calling someone a liar.

The procedures for civil contempt are described in detail in Mass. R. Civ. P. 65.3. A civil contempt proceeding is commenced by filing a complaint for contempt with the court whose injunction you claim has been violated. The complaint for contempt must

- include a verbatim statement of the injunction or order involved,

- identify the court that issued the injunction or order,

- contain the case caption and docket number of the case in which the injunction or order was filed,

- include a short statement of facts on which the asserted contempt is based,

- include a prayer for the issuance of a summons,

- be verified or supported by affidavits, and

- otherwise comply with the provisions of Mass. R. Civ. P. 8–11.

No entry fee is required in connection with filing a complaint for contempt.

The summons issues only on a judge's order and directs the parties to appear before the court not later than ten days thereafter for the purpose of scheduling a trial, considering whether the filing of an answer is necessary, holding a hearing on the merits of the complaint, or considering other matters that the court deems appropriate. Mass. R. Civ. P. 65.3(d). Service must be in hand unless the court authorizes an alternative method. Mass. R. Civ. P. 65.3(e).

"[A] civil contempt finding [must] be supported by clear and convincing evidence of disobedience of a clear and convincing command." *In re Birchall*, 454 Mass. 837, 853 (2009). Where an injunction is in effect, "the party bound by the order is responsible for ascertaining whether any proposed actions are among the proscribed activities." *Demoulas v. Demoulas Super Mkts., Inc.*, 424 Mass. at 569. "[I]t is not the plaintiff's obligation to police the decree but the defendant's obligation to make certain he does not violate it. Thus if the defendant saw the decree as ambiguous on the point in question, he could have sought clarification from the court before he engaged in the questionable conduct." *Coyne Indus. Laundry of Schenectady, Inc. v. Gould*, 359 Mass. 269, 275–76 (1971).

Because the purpose of civil contempt proceedings is remedial, the formulation of the remedy is within the judge's discretion. *Demoulas v. Demoulas Super Mkts., Inc.*, 424 Mass. at 571. Often, a court will order both damages and attorney fees, *see Eldim, Inc. v. Mullen*, 47 Mass. App. Ct. 125, 129–30 (1999), and even incarceration to coerce compliance is a possibility. Both sides should treat a contempt proceeding with the seriousness it deserves.

In certain circumstances, you may want to consider a complaint for criminal contempt pursuant to Mass. R. Crim. P. 44. *Furtado v. Furtado*, 380 Mass. 137, 141–43 (1980). While a civil contempt is remedial in nature, a criminal contempt is punitive. In contrast to a civil contempt finding, a criminal contempt conviction will stand even if the underlying injunction or order is subsequently overturned. Unlike a civil contempt proceeding, however, criminal contempt must be proven "beyond a reasonable doubt." *Furtado v. Furtado*, 380 Mass. at 142.

CHAPTER 7

Seeking Injunctive Relief in Particular Situations

Brandon F. White, Esq.
Foley Hoag LLP, Boston

§ 7.1   Enforcement of Employee Noncompetition Agreements................... 7–1
  § 7.1.1   Enforceability of the Noncompetition Agreement 7–2
  § 7.1.2   Costs and Benefits of Litigation 7–3
  § 7.1.3   Settlement 7–4
  § 7.1.4   Protective Order 7–4
  § 7.1.5   Determining Who the Defendants Should Be 7–5
  § 7.1.6   Injunction Bonds 7–5
  § 7.1.7   Documents in the Possession of the Former Employee 7–5
§ 7.2   Enforcement of Statutes by the Attorney General 7–5
EXHIBIT 7A—Confidentiality Stipulation 7–7

The need for immediate injunctive relief arises in myriad situations. The guidelines described above should apply to most cases where your client is seeking a TRO or preliminary injunction. The following discussion addresses two particular situations where the need for immediate injunctive relief arises: the enforcement of employee noncompetition agreements and the enforcement of various statutory provisions by the Massachusetts Office of the Attorney General.

§ 7.1   ENFORCEMENT OF EMPLOYEE NONCOMPETITION AGREEMENTS

Noncompetition agreements are common features of many employment agreements. Because employers and employees often have fundamentally different views as to the scope and enforceability of such agreements, lawsuits frequently result, and Superior Court judges are required to consider the parties' conflicting interests.

Judicial Commentary
If the judge is going to grant relief, it serves the interests of both parties for the order to be narrow enough so as not to deprive anyone of a livelihood. Otherwise, the order may be very vulnerable on an interlocutory appeal.

A preliminary injunction is the single most important remedy in a case seeking enforcement of an employee noncompetition agreement. There are several reasons for this. First, in the absence of a preliminary injunction, the request for specific enforcement of the noncompetition agreement may become moot. *All Stainless, Inc. v.*

Colby, 364 Mass. 773, 781 (1974). Second, if the former employer seeks to protect its trade secrets or customer goodwill, immediate relief is essential. Finally, a preliminary injunction has substantial precedential and psychological effect and will often control the ultimate outcome of the litigation.

In dealing with motions for preliminary injunctive relief in these disputes, counsel for the parties must address a number of issues.

§ 7.1.1   Enforceability of the Noncompetition Agreement

Whether you represent the plaintiff–former employer or the defendant–former employee, you should carefully investigate the facts and applicable law and determine whether the noncompetition agreement is enforceable under the particular facts of your case. Under the Massachusetts Noncompetition Agreement Act, G.L. c. 149, § 24L, a noncompetition agreement must at a minimum meet the following requirements:

- it must be no broader than necessary to protect a legitimate business interests of the employer;

- it must not exceed twelve months, unless the employee breached their fiduciary duty or took property belonging to the employer, in which case it may not exceed two years;

- it must be reasonable in geographic scope and scope of proscribed activities; and

- it is consonant with public policy.

Legitimate business interests include the protection of trade secrets, confidential business information, and customer goodwill. G.L. c. 149, § 24L(b)(iii); *see also Marine Contractors Co. v. Hurley*, 365 Mass. 280, 287 (1974). Because noncompetition agreements are enforceable only to the extent necessary to protect legitimate business interests, courts will not enforce such agreements when the purported trade secret or confidential information is not in fact confidential. *See, e.g., Patriot Energy Grp., Inc. v. Kiley*, 32 Mass. L. Rptr. 169 (Mass. Super. Ct. Feb. 25, 2014).

A geographic reach that is limited to only the geographic areas in which the employee, during the last two years of employment, provided services or had a presence is presumptively reasonable. G.L. c. 149, § 24L(b)(v). But Massachusetts courts have also found noncompetition agreements with large, even nationwide, geographic scopes reasonable so long as they coincide with the area in which the plaintiff performs business. *See Marine Contractors Co. v. Hurley*, 365 Mass. 280, 289 (1974); *Rentex, Inc. v. Franco*, 35 Mass. L. Rptr. 183 (Mass. Super. Ct. July 12, 2018).

An agreement is presumptively reasonable in scope if it is limited only to the specific types of services provided by the employee at any time during the last two years of employment. G.L. c. 149, § 24L(b)(vi).

In addition, a court may, in its discretion, revise a noncompetition agreement so as to render it valid and enforceable. G.L. c. 149, § 24L(d). For example, numerous Massachusetts decisions have enforced noncompetition agreements of two to three years' duration, and courts may employ the blue pencil doctrine to modify agreements that are overly restrictive in their geographic or temporal scope. *All Stainless, Inc. v. Colby*, 364 Mass. 773, 777 (1974). By blue penciling, courts allow agreements to be enforced to the extent they are reasonable rather than finding them unenforceable in their entirety. But a court will not rewrite an agreement to the extent that it may change the nature of the bargain. *Hurwitz Grp., Inc. v. Ptak*, 2002 Mass. Super. LEXIS 565, at *13 (Mass. Super. Ct. June 27, 2002).

In addition to considering whether the agreement protects legitimate business interests and is reasonable in scope, you should review other possible legal defenses, including whether the agreement is supported by a garden leave clause or other mutually agreed upon consideration, whether the employer has breached the agreement, whether the agreement complies with the procedural requirements of G.L. c. 149, § 24L(b)(i) and (ii), and whether the agreement was induced by fraud or duress. The equitable defenses of laches and unclean hands also need to be considered.

Often the defendant can argue persuasively that the plaintiff itself engages in the same kind of acquisitive or competitive conduct about which it is complaining. Strictly speaking, this may not constitute unclean hands if it did not involve the particular defendant, but it is worthwhile for the defendant to point out this kind of inconsistency or hypocrisy on the part of one seeking equitable relief. After you have determined the enforceability of the noncompetition agreement—or at least assessed the likelihood of enforcement—you will be in a position to develop a winning litigation strategy.

Ethics Commentary

Noncompetition agreements between attorneys are generally unethical, except for provisions concerning retirement benefits. Mass. R. Prof. C. 5.6(a). The rationale of this rule is that a client is not a widget and always has a right to select their counsel of choice. *See also* Mass. R. Prof. C. 5.6(a) cmt. [1].

Noncompetition agreements are not enforceable against employees classified as nonexempt under the Fair Labor Standards Act; undergraduate or graduate students who partake in an internship or short-term employment; employees terminated without cause or laid off; or employees age eighteen or younger. G.L. c. 149, § 24L(c).

§ 7.1.2   Costs and Benefits of Litigation

Litigation regarding the enforceability of noncompetition agreements can be expensive, both in legal fees and time. If you represent the former employer, you should consider whether the potential benefits of the litigation warrant the inevitable costs. For example, if the likelihood of enforcement is low, do you want to risk a bad precedent and the message that such a precedent may send to your remaining employees? If you represent the former employee, you may have a limited litigation budget and your client may not want to adopt an "all or nothing" strategy.

§ 7.1.3   Settlement

Because of the substantial costs of litigation in this area and the difficulty in accurately predicting preliminary injunction rulings by Superior Court judges, litigants should consider compromising their respective positions. In many instances, the legitimate needs of the former employer can be satisfied while at the same time allowing the former employee to pursue gainful employment, albeit with some restrictions. For example, the employer might agree to reduce the geographic scope of the noncompetition agreement from all six New England states to Massachusetts or reduce the temporal scope of the agreement from two years to six months. Many Superior Court judges expect counsel for the parties to have explored settlement *before* the preliminary injunction hearing.

> **Practice Note**
> If you represent the former employer, beware of delays that may be caused by any settlement negotiations. If the negotiations fail, the former employee may claim that a preliminary injunction should not issue because of the employer's delay in commencing a lawsuit. *See Alexander & Alexander, Inc. v. Danahy*, 21 Mass. App. Ct. 488, 494–95 (1986) ("Unexplained delay in seeking relief for allegedly wrongful conduct may indicate an absence of irreparable harm and may make an injunction based upon that conduct inappropriate."). If you represent the former employee, you should be wary in acknowledging the enforceability of the agreement in any settlement negotiations. While statements made in settlement negotiations are generally inadmissible as evidence, the opposing party may seek to use such an acknowledgment as a damaging admission if settlement is not reached.

§ 7.1.4   Protective Order

If trade secrets or confidential business information are involved, the former employer should make sure that the Superior Court judge enters an appropriate protective order pursuant to Mass. R. Civ. P. 26(c). *Beck v. Fid. Nat'l Ins. Co.*, 27 Mass. L. Rptr. 176 (Mass. Super. Ct. 2010). Otherwise, the employer will risk the loss of its valuable proprietary information. Often, the parties are able to agree on a confidentiality stipulation, which will then be entered as a court order. See **Exhibit 7A**. Such a confidentiality stipulation usually includes the following:

- a mechanism for designating "confidential" information and documents,

- identification of the individuals who will be allowed access to the confidential material,

- limitations on the use of the confidential material, and

- a provision requiring the return of all confidential material at the conclusion of the litigation.

The Massachusetts Trial Court's Uniform Rules on Impoundment Procedure apply to any "confidential" documents filed with the court with a request for impoundment.

§ 7.1.5   Determining Who the Defendants Should Be

Sometimes it is better not to sue the new employer. The new employer may have a deeper pocket and may invest more resources in the defense of the lawsuit. The new employer may be able to rely on defenses (e.g., lack of personal jurisdiction) that are unavailable to the former employee. In many cases, however, it is important to name the new employer as a defendant. The new employer, unlike the former employee, is likely to have the financial resources to pay any damages award, and discovery is measurably easier if the new employer is a party.

§ 7.1.6   Injunction Bonds

The issue of security should be discussed with your client whether you represent the former employer or the former employee. The former employer should be warned that an injunction bond will likely be required in the event the preliminary injunction issues. The former employee should determine what amount of security should be requested from the court. The amount of security generally is tailored to approximate the employee's lost earnings and other anticipated damages during the period of the injunction.

§ 7.1.7   Documents in the Possession of the Former Employee

A recurring issue is the former employee's retention of documents belonging to the former employer. In many instances, documents are retained quite innocently by the former employee. In some cases, however, the former employee intentionally retains confidential and proprietary documents and plans to use them on behalf of the new employer. If you represent the former employee, you should consider counseling your client to immediately return all such confidential and proprietary documents to the former employer, unless you have a good defense to a claim for the wrongful taking and retention of those documents.

Once litigation has been threatened or commenced, the former employee should not destroy or delete any documents in their possession, including documents belonging to the former employer. Such action could constitute spoliation and subject the client or attorney to sanctions.

§ 7.2   ENFORCEMENT OF STATUTES BY THE ATTORNEY GENERAL

The Massachusetts attorney general may seek preliminary injunctive relief in connection with the enforcement of numerous statutes. There are two key differences between injunctive relief sought by private litigants and injunctive relief sought by the attorney general. First, in actions commenced by the attorney general, the public interest is always a factor that should be considered by the court. Second, the attorney general is not required to demonstrate irreparable harm when seeking preliminary injunctive relief to prevent violation of a statute. *Commonwealth v. Mass. CRINC*, 392 Mass. 79, 89 (1984).

The attorney general is expressly authorized by statute to seek injunctive relief in a number of areas, including the following:

- **Civil rights.** The attorney general may bring a civil action for injunctive relief to protect "the peaceable exercise or enjoyment" of a person's constitutional rights, either under the U.S. or Massachusetts Constitutions. G.L. c. 12, § 11H.

- **Consumer protection.** The attorney general may bring a civil action "to restrain by temporary restraining order or preliminary or permanent injunction" unfair competition or unfair or deceptive business practices. Violation of such an injunction may result in a civil penalty of not more than $10,000 for each such violation. G.L. c. 93A, § 4.

- **Environmental protection.** The attorney general may bring an action for injunctive relief against any person violating G.L. c. 21 or any order or regulation promulgated under G.L. c. 21. G.L. c. 21, § 46. This statute governs the Department of Environmental Management, including the divisions of forests and parks, marine fisheries, fisheries and wildlife, water resources, conservation services, water pollution control, and mineral resources. The attorney general also may petition the Superior Court to enjoin violations of the Hazardous Waste Management Act. Any violation of the act "shall be presumed to constitute irreparable harm to the public health, welfare, safety and to the environment." G.L. c. 21C, § 10.

- **Public charities.** The attorney general may bring an action in the Superior Court to restrain a public charity from failing to register with the attorney general's Division of Public Charities and to restrain a public charity from transacting any business while remaining unregistered. G.L. c. 12, § 8E. The attorney general is authorized to seek injunctive relief to prevent misappropriation of funds by public charities. G.L. c. 12, § 8. The attorney general also is authorized to seek injunctions to prevent public charities from engaging in fraud or other deceptive conduct. G.L. c. 68, § 32(e).

- **Administrative law.** The attorney general may seek injunctive relief to compel a person to comply with a regulation or directive of a state agency. G.L. c. 214, § 3(12).

EXHIBIT 7A—Confidentiality Stipulation

COMMONWEALTH OF MASSACHUSETTS

MIDDLESEX, ss.   SUPERIOR COURT
                                        CIVIL ACTION NO.

COMPUTER SOFTWARE, INC., Plaintiff	))))
v.	))
HARRY ADAMS and KOPY SOFTWARE, INC.,	))
Defendants	)))

STIPULATION AND ORDER REGARDING CONFIDENTIAL
INFORMATION AND DOCUMENTS PRODUCED
DURING DISCOVERY

It is hereby stipulated by the attorneys for the parties, subject to the approval of the Court, as follows:

1. Financial, proprietary, technical or other confidential and sensitive business information produced by any party in this litigation, the disclosure of which that party feels could reasonably be anticipated either to cause competitive injury to the party producing the information or to cause injury to the current or future business relations of that party, may be designated as "Confidential Material" by such party in the manner described in Paragraph 3, below. Such information includes, but is not limited to, the following subjects: financial statements; income statements; tax returns; source code; object code; customer lists and related customer information; supplier lists and related supplier information; price information; sales information; trade secrets, and any other confidential, financial, proprietary or other sensitive business information. "Confidential Material" shall also include all documents and things, including tapes and disks, containing portions of confidential information, extracts therefrom, or summaries thereof.

2. This Stipulation and Order Regarding Confidential Information and Documents Produced During Discovery (the "Stipulation and Order") shall apply to (a) all information, documents and things requested or provided in this action, including, without limitation: testimony adduced and documents or things marked as exhibits at depositions upon oral examination or upon written questions pursuant to the Massachusetts Rules of Civil Procedure

Rules 30 and 31; answers to interrogatories pursuant to Mass. R. Civ. P. 33, documents and things produced pursuant to Mass. R. Civ. P. 34, and answers to requests for admissions pursuant to Mass. R. Civ. P. 36 and (b) documents and things voluntarily transferred between counsel for the parties in connection with this action.

3. Confidential Material may be used or disclosed only in accordance with this Stipulation and Order. Documents or information may be designated as Confidential Material within the meaning of this Stipulation and Order in the following ways:

(a) Each interrogatory answer or portion thereof, each produced or transferred document or thing or portion thereof, and each answer to a request for admission or portion thereof that is deemed by a party to disclose Confidential Material of that party shall be so identified, and clearly and prominently labeled by that party as "CONFIDENTIAL," or with a phrase that includes the word "CONFIDENTIAL."

(b) In the case of answers to interrogatories and requests for admissions, memoranda, or other documents served and the information contained therein, designation shall also be made by placing the following legend clearly and prominently on the front of any set of interrogatory answers, responses to requests for admissions, or other documents or things containing Confidential Material: "CONTAINS CONFIDENTIAL MATERIAL. Designated parts not to be used, copied or disclosed, except as authorized by Order of the Middlesex Superior Court, Civil Action No. _____."

(c) In the case of depositions and the information contained therein (including exhibits), designation of the portion of the transcript (including exhibits) that contains Confidential Material shall be made by a statement to such effect, on the record, and during the course of the deposition, by counsel for the party producing such information, or shall be made by advising opposing counsel in writing, within fourteen (14) days after the receipt of the deposition transcript, of the specific pages and lines or exhibits to be treated as Confidential Material. The following legend shall be placed on the front of any deposition transcript containing Confidential Material: "CONTAINS CONFIDENTIAL MATERIAL. Designated parts not to be used, copied or disclosed, except as authorized by Order of the Middlesex Superior Court, Civil Action No. _____."

(d) When any testimony in this action is taken, counsel for any party may, before or during said testimony, give notice to counsel for all other parties that Confidential Material may be disclosed during said testimony, and such counsel may require that the testimony go forward with only the court stenographer recording the testimony, and those categories of persons listed in Paragraphs 5 or 6, below, in attendance. In any testimony in which the notice provided for in the preceding sentence is given, or in which any item of information, document or thing marked or identified as Confidential Material in accordance with Paragraph 3, hereof, is presented, disclosed or marked for identification, the court stenographer recording the testimony, and all other persons who are attending such testimony at the time of such presentation, disclosure or marking, shall be deemed persons to whom access to and disclosure of such item of information, document or thing is permitted, but all such persons shall be subject to the provisions of this Stipulation and Order. The stenotype tape or other means of recording the proceedings with respect to which the notice provided for in this Paragraph is given, or in which any Confidential Material marked or identified in accordance with this Stipulation and Order is disclosed, presented or marked for identification, shall itself be deemed Confidential Material subject to this Stipulation and Order. The transcript and/or copies thereof of any such testimony shall be provided by the aforesaid court stenographer only to counsel of record in this action. At any deposition where Confidential Material is disclosed, the court stenographer shall read this Stipulation and Order and sign the Agreement to Be Bound by Protective Order, attached hereto as Exhibit A.

4. Two types of Confidential Material may be designated: "Highly Confidential" and "Confidential."

5. "Highly Confidential" Material may be disclosed only to the persons identified in subparagraphs (a) through (d) hereof, solely for the purpose of conducting this particular action, and not for conducting any other case or for any business or other purpose whatsoever, under the procedures set forth in this Stipulation and Order. The persons to whom "Highly Confidential" Material may be disclosed are as follows:

    (a) Partners, associate attorneys, and secretarial and paralegal personnel of the firms of _____ and _____;

    (b) Expert witnesses retained by or assisting the attorneys of record in preparation for trial, trial, or appeal of this action, including consulting and testifying expert witnesses, subject to the conditions of Paragraph 8, below;

    (c) Deposition reporters in the course of their work in this action; and

    (d) Court personnel in the course of their work in this action.

6. "Confidential" Material may be disclosed only to the persons identified in subparagraphs (a) through (f) hereof, solely for the purpose of conducting this particular action, and not for conducting any other case or for any business or other purpose whatsoever, under the procedures set forth in this Stipulation and Order. The persons to whom "Confidential" Material may be disclosed are as follows:

(a) Partners, associate attorneys, and secretarial and paralegal personnel of the firms of _____ and _____;

(b) Expert witnesses retained by or assisting the attorneys of record in preparation for trial, trial, or appeal of this action, including consulting and testifying expert witnesses, subject to the conditions of Paragraph 8, below;

(c) The parties to this action and their officers, directors and employees;

(d) Witnesses and their counsel in this action;

(e) Deposition reporters in the course of their work in this action; and

(f) Court personnel in the course of their work in this action.

7. Only attorneys of record may authorize the disclosure of information designated by a party as Highly Confidential Material or Confidential Material to a person described in Paragraphs 5 or 6, above. Prior to disclosure in any manner or form, directly or indirectly, in substance or otherwise, of any information designated by a party as Highly Confidential Material or Confidential Material to any person described in Paragraphs 5 or 6, above, such person shall first be advised that such information is being disclosed pursuant and subject to the terms of this Stipulation and Order, and may not be disclosed in any manner or form, either directly or indirectly, in substance or otherwise, to any other person; and that the information, and all copies thereof, must remain in the person's custody until returned to the attorney of record, and must be returned to the attorney of record upon completion of its use by the person; and such person, except for any such person identified in subparagraphs 5(a), 5(d), 6(a) and 6(f), shall have executed the Agreement to Be Bound by Protective Order, attached hereto as Exhibit A. A copy of each such executed Agreement to be Bound by Protective Order shall be forwarded to all attorneys of record for the parties to this action immediately upon its execution.

8. Before any Highly Confidential Material or Confidential Material is disclosed to any expert witness, the party that designated the information as Highly Confidential or Confidential shall be given ten (10) days' prior notice, in writing, of the person or persons to whom disclosure is to be made, and of the Highly Confidential or Confidential information that is to be disclosed. Said notice shall identify the full name, employer, position and business address of the expert witness, and shall identify any prior business or other relationship with the retaining party. The party that designated the information as Highly Confidential or Confidential may, within such ten (10)-day period, seek a protective order to prevent disclosure of the information to the proposed person. No disclosure shall be made to such person prior to the expiration of such period, or, if a motion for a protective order is filed, prior to the Court's ruling on such motion.

9. The Highly Confidential Material and Confidential Material shall be used by any person to whom it is disclosed pursuant to Paragraphs 5 and 6, above, solely in connection with and for purposes of preparation for trial, trial, or appeal of this action.

10. Any interrogatory answers, answers to requests for admissions, briefs, memoranda, depositions and affidavits (including exhibits), or any other document or paper containing or referencing Confidential Material that is submitted or presented to, or filed with, the Court, shall be submitted in a sealed envelope bearing the caption of this action and containing the following notice:

> Documents Subject to Protective Order. This envelope contains documents filed under a Protective Order. It is not to be opened other than by the Court, nor are the contents hereof to be displayed or revealed other than to the Court, except by Court order or agreement of the parties.

Said envelope shall be maintained by the Clerk of the Court under seal, and shall not be available to persons other than the Court or persons authorized to have access to such Confidential Material by this Order.

11. A party may, subject to the rules of evidence, use any information designated as Confidential Material for any purpose at trial or at any hearing before a judicial officer, provided that notice is given to counsel for the party producing the Confidential Material, and provided further that such counsel may at the time of such proposed use, and prior to the disclosure of the Confidential Material, move for an appropriate protective order. In the event that any Confidential Material is used in any court proceeding herein, it shall not lose its confidential status through such use, and the parties shall take all steps reasonably required to protect its confidentiality during such use.

12. With respect to any particular item of Confidential Material, the restrictions on dissemination, access, disclosure and use of such item or of information contained therein provided for herein shall not apply to the party who identified or marked such item as confidential in accordance with this Stipulation and Order or to such party's attorneys.

13. Acceptance by a receiving party of information, documents or things identified or marked as Confidential Material hereunder by a disclosing party shall not constitute a concession that such information, documents or things in fact are or include Confidential Material of such disclosing party.

14. Within thirty (30) days after the final termination of this litigation as to any party, all documents and things in that party's possession that contain Confidential Material produced by another party, and all copies thereof, shall be returned to counsel for the party who produced them. For purposes of this Paragraph, the final termination of a case as to any party may be by settlement, by a judgment that has become nonappealable, or by a final disposition on appeal.

15. Nothing contained in this Stipulation and Order shall be deemed to restrict any party from using or disclosing in any manner whatsoever, information, documents or other materials obtained by that party in a manner other than pursuant to any discovery in this litigation.

16. Nothing contained in this Stipulation and Order shall affect the right, if any, of any party to make any other type of objection, claim or other response to interrogatories, requests for production of documents, requests for admissions, or any questions at a deposition. Nor shall this Stipulation and Order be construed as a waiver by any party of any legally cognizable privilege to withhold any document or information, or of any right any party may have to assert such privilege at any stage of the proceeding.

17. This Stipulation and Order shall not prevent a party from applying to the Court for further or additional protective orders, or from agreeing to modification of this Stipulation and Order, subject to the approval of the Court.

18. This Stipulation and Order shall survive the entry of judgment in this action or any stipulation of dismissal thereof, and shall remain in force and effect until modified, superseded or terminated by written consent of the parties, or by order of the Court made upon reasonable written request.

19. All notices given by counsel for one party to counsel for any other party under this Stipulation and Order shall be delivered by hand, by telecopier, or by overnight mail.

20. This Stipulation may be entered as an Order of the Court by consent of the parties and shall be binding on the parties as of the date signed by the parties.

COMPUTER SOFTWARE, INC.

By its Attorneys,

HARRY ADAMS and KOPY SOFTWARE, INC.

By their Attorneys,

_____
Attorney(s) (BBO No. XXXXXX)
Firm Name
Address
Phone

_____
Attorney(s) (BBO No. XXXXXX)
Firm Name
Address
Phone

Dated: _____

APPROVED BY THE COURT:

Dated: _____

_____
(_____, J.)

EXHIBIT A

COMMONWEALTH OF MASSACHUSETTS

MIDDLESEX, ss.   SUPERIOR COURT
                                                            CIVIL ACTION NO.

```
_____
                                )
[NAME],                         )
                Plaintiff       )
                                )
v.                              )
                                )
[NAME],                         )
                Defendants      )
_____ )
```

AGREEMENT TO BE BOUND BY PROTECTIVE ORDER

1. My name is _____. I live at _____. I am employed as (state position) _____ by _____ (state name, address and telephone number of employer).

2. I am aware that a Stipulation and Order Regarding Confidential Information and Documents Produced During Discovery (the "Stipulation and Order") has been entered in the above-captioned litigation in the Middlesex Superior Court. A copy of the Stipulation and Order has been given to me and I have carefully read and understand same.

3. I have had no prior relationship or dealings with, or ownership interest in, any of the parties in this case or their affiliates, except _____. (If none, state "None.")

4. I am not currently employed by or provide consulting or other services to any person, corporation or other entity that is directly competitive with any of the parties in this case, except _____. (If none, state "None.")

5. I promise and agree that documents and information designated as Confidential Material under the Stipulation and Order entered in the above case will be used by me only under and in accordance with the terms of the Stipulation and Order.

6. I promise and agree that I will not disclose or discuss Confidential Material with any person other than those persons specifically listed in the Stipulation and Order, and under the procedures therein specified.

7. I understand that any use or disclosure of Confidential Material, or any portions or summaries thereof, or any information obtained therefrom in any manner contrary to the provisions of the Stipulation and Order, will subject me to personal liability and the sanctions of the Court.

_____
(Signature)

Sworn to and subscribed before me this _____ day of _____, 20__.

_____
Notary Public

Table of Cases

References are to section numbers of this book, unless otherwise indicated.

A

A-Copy, Inc. v. Michaelson, 4.3
Alexander & Alexander, Inc. v. Danahy, 2.3, 7.1.3
All Stainless, Inc. v. Colby, 1.4, 7.1, 7.1.1

B

Bank of New Eng. v. Mortgage Corp. of New Eng., 1.3
Beck v. Fidelity Nat'l Ins. Co., 7.1.4
Birchall, In re, 6.4
Boston Police Patrolmen's Ass'n, Inc. v. Police Dep't of Bos., 1.3
Boston Select Grp., Inc. v. Ristaino, 2.2
Brookline v. Goldstein, 2.3

C

Coyne Indus. Laundry of Schenectady, Inc. v. Gould, 6.4

D

Demoulas Super Mkts., Inc. v. Peter's Mkt. Basket, 6.3, 6.4

E

Edwin R. Sage Co. v. Foley, 6.3
Eldim, Inc. v. Mullen, 6.4

F

Farley v. Sprague, 2.3
Fleet Nat'l Bank v. Rapid Reprocessing Co., Inc., 1.3
Fonar Corp. v. Deccaid Servs., 2.4
Fremont Inv. & Loan, Commonwealth v., 6.3
French v. Vandkjaer, 2.3
Furtado v. Furtado, 6.4

G

Garcia v. Department of Hous. & Cmty. Dev., 1.3
Griffith, In re, 5.1

H

Helmes v. Commonwealth, 6.3

Hull Mun. Lighting Plant v. Massachusetts Mun. Wholesale Elec. Co., 1.3, 1.4
Hurwitz Grp., Inc. v. Ptak, 7.1.1

J

Joyce, In re, 1.4

L

Loyal Order of Moose, Inc. v. Board of Health of Yarmouth, 6.3

M

Mahlowitz, In re, 5.1
Marine Contractors Co. v. Hurley, 7.1.1
Massachusetts CRINC, Commonwealth v., 7.2
McCarthy, In re, 2.3

N

Norfolk Cty. Hosp. v. Commonwealth, 1.3

O

O'Day v. Theran, 1.4

P

Packaging Indus. Grp., Inc. v. Cheney, 1.3, 2.4, 6.3
Patriot Energy Grp., Inc. v. Kiley, 7.1.1
Paypal, Inc. v. NantHealth, Inc., 1.3
PC-Plus Techs., Inc. v. Gokani, 1.4
Planned Parenthood League of Mass., Inc. v. Operation Rescue, 1.3, 2.2, 2.3
Plastic Surgical Servs., P.C. v. Hall, 2.4

R

Rentex, Inc. v. Franco, 7.1.1

S

Sax v. Sax, 2.4
Silva v. Romney, 5.1

T

Thayer Co. v. Binnall, 4.4
Tri-Nel Mgmt., Inc. v. Board of Health, 1.3

Table of Statutes, Rules, and References

References are to section numbers of this book, unless otherwise indicated.

MASSACHUSETTS

Hazardous Waste Management Act, 7.2

Massachusetts Attorney Discipline Reports (Mass. Att'y Disc. R.)
9 Mass. Att'y Disc. R. 394, 2.3
11 Mass. Att'y Disc. R. 373, 2.3
16 Mass. Att'y Disc. R. 447, 2.3

Massachusetts General Laws (G.L. c.)
c. 12
  § 8, 7.2
  § 8E, 7.2
  § 11H, 7.2
c. 21, 7.2
  § 46, 7.2
c. 21C, § 10, 7.2
c. 21E, 2.2
c. 68, § 32(e), 7.2
c. 93
  § 42, Exhibit 2A
  § 42A, Exhibit 2A
c. 93A, 2.2, Exhibit 2A
  § 1, Exhibit 2A
  § 4, 7.2
  § 11, Exhibit 2A
c. 149
  § 24L, 7.1.1
  § 24L(b)(i), 7.1.1
  § 24L(b)(ii), 7.1.1
  § 24L(b)(iii), 7.1.1
  § 24L(b)(v), 7.1.1
  § 24L(b)(vi), 7.1.1
  § 24L(c), 7.1.1
  § 24L(d), 7.1.1
c. 214
  § 3(12), 7.2
c. 231
  § 118, 6.3
c. 268, § 1A, 2.3

Massachusetts Noncompetition Agreement Act, 7.1.1

Massachusetts Rules of Civil Procedure (Mass. R. Civ. P.)
Rule 4(c), 2.7, Exhibit 2C
Rule 6(c), 4.3
Rule 7(b)(1), 2.4
Rules 8–11, 6.4
Rule 26(c), 7.1.4
Rule 30, Exhibit 7A
Rule 31, Exhibit 7A
Rule 33, Exhibit 7A
Rule 34, Exhibit 7A
Rule 36, Exhibit 7A
Rule 38(d), 2.2
Rule 65, 2.4
Rule 65(a), 1.5, Exhibit 1A
Rule 65(b), Exhibit 1B
Rule 65(b)(1), 1.5
Rule 65(b)(2), 1.4
Rule 65(c), 1.4, 5.1, 6.2
Rule 65(d), 2.4
Rule 65.3, 6.4
Rule 65.3(d), 6.4
Rule 65.3(e), 6.4

Massachusetts Rules of Criminal Procedure (Mass. R. Crim. P.)
Rule 44, 6.4

Massachusetts Rules of Professional Conduct (Mass. R. Prof. C.), 8.7
Rule 1.2(a), 5.1
Rule 1.4(a), 5.1
Rule 3.1, 5.1
Rule 3.3(a)(2), 6.2
Rule 3.3(a)(3), 4.4
Rule 3.4(c), 6.2
Rule 3.5(a), 2.4
Rule 3.5(b), 2.4
Rule 4.3, 4.1
Rule 4.3(a), 4.1
Rule 4.3(b), 4.1
Rule 5.6(a), 7.1.1
Rule 8.4(c), 2.3

Superior Court Rules (Super. Ct. R.)
Rule 9A, 2.4, 2.6
Rule 9A(a)(1), 2.5
Rule 9A(a)(5), 2.5
Rule 9A(c)(3), 2.4
Rule 9A(e)(1), 2.4, 2.6, Exhibit 2B
Rule 15, 2.3, 7.1.4
Rule 20, 2.2, 7.1.4, 8.1.1, 8.2.1

Superior Court Standing Orders
1-88, Exhibits 1A, 1B, 2A, 2C, 2B

UNIFORM RULES, ABA MODEL RULES, AND OTHER ABA SOURCES

Uniform Rules on Impoundment Procedure, 7.1.4

ADDITIONAL REFERENCES AND RESOURCES

Xifaras, M.D., "The Attorney-Client Relationship," *Ethical Lawyering in Massachusetts*, ch. 4 (MCLE, Inc. 5th ed. 2021), 1.2

Index

References are to section numbers of this book, unless otherwise indicated.

A

Affidavits
Basis of, 2.3, 4.3
Opposing
Preliminary injunction, 4.3
Supporting
Verified complaints, 2.1, 2.2, 2.3

Affirmative Defenses, 3.3.2, 13.2.3(b)

Appeal
Preliminary injunction, of, 6.3

Attorney General, 7.2

Attorneys
Employee noncompetition agreements, 7.1.1

C

Civil Action Cover Sheet, 3.1

Civil Clerks, 3.1

Civil Rights Cases, 7.2

Clients
Communication with, 4.1, 5.1
Preliminary injunction hearings, presence at, 5.1

Complaints, 3.1
Cover sheet, 3.1
Injunctive relief, verified complaint, Exhibit 2A
Jury demand, 2.2
Preliminary injunctions, for, 2.1, 2.2
TROs, for, 2.2
Verified, 2.2

Confidentiality
Injunctive relief, confidentiality stipulation, Exhibit 7A

Cover Sheets, 3.1

Cross-Examination
Affidavits in, 2.3

D

Department of Environmental Management, 7.2

E

Employee Noncompetition Agreements, 7.1

Equity Clerks, 3.1

F

Filing Fees, 3.1

G

Good Faith by Attorney, 2.3

H

Hearings
Preliminary injunction, motion for, 2.4, 5.1

I

Injunction Bonds
Employee noncompetition disputes, 7.1.6

Injunctions, Motions for, 2.1, 2.4
See also Temporary Restraining Orders (TROs)
Appealing, 6.3
Confidentiality stipulation, Exhibit 7A
Decision to seek, 1.1, 1.4
Documents filed with
Affidavits for, 2.3
Complaints, 3.2.5, 2.1, 2.2
Memorandum supporting motion for, 2.1, 2.5
Motion for short order of notice, 2.6
Motion for special process server, 2.7
Proposed order, 2.1, 2.4
Employee noncompetition agreement enforcement, for, 7.1
Enforcement of, 6.4
Execution of, 6.2
Filing, 3.1
Hearings, 2.4, 5.1
Investigation before filing, 1.2
Opposing
Affidavits, 4.3
Memorandum, 4.4
Preparation for, 4.1
Standstill agreements, 4.2
Posthearing, Chapter 6

Injunction Bonds *(cont'd)*
Preliminary injunctions, Exhibit 1B
Prior to decision, actions, 6.1
Standard for relief, 1.3, 1.5
Statutory provisions for, 7.2
Verified complaint, Exhibit 2A

Inquiry by Attorney
Motion for preliminary injunction, before
    filing, 1.2

J

Jury Demand
In complaint, 2.2

M

Memoranda of Law
Opposing motions for preliminary injunction,
    4.4
Supporting motions
    Preliminary injunction, for, 2.1, 2.5

O

Oral Advocacy
Preliminary injunction hearings, at, 5.1

Orders
Proposed, 9.15
    Preliminary injunctions, 2.1, 2.4

P

Parties
Employee noncompetition disputes, 7.1.5

Pro Se Litigants
Preliminary injunction hearings, 4.1

Protective Order, Motions for
Employee noncompetition disputes, 7.1.4

S

Security
Alternatives means of, 1.4
Preliminary injunctions, 5.1

Security Bonds
For preliminary injunctions, 1.4, 6.2

Service
Preliminary injunction
    Memorandum, 2.5
    Opposition affidavits, 4.3
    Opposition memoranda, 4.4
    Orders, 6.2

Session Clerks
Filing for injunction, 3.1

Settlement
Employee noncompetition disputes, 7.1.3

Short Order of Notice, Motions for, 2.1, 2.6,
3.1, Exhibit 2B

Signature
Client, 2.3

Special Process Server, Motions for
Preliminary injunction
    Motions, 2.1, 2.7, 3.1, Exhibit 2C
Preliminary injunctions
    Orders, 6.2

Standstill Agreements, 4.2, Exhibit 4A

Stipulations
Injunctive relief, confidentiality stipulation,
    Exhibit 7A

T

Temporary Restraining Orders (TROs)
Complaints, 2.2
Motions, Exhibit 1A
Need for, 1.5
Preliminary injunctions compared, 1.5
Standard for relief, 1.5

V

Verified Complaints, 2.2

W

Witnesses
Identification of, 4.1